Mind Your Language

Mind Your Language!

✦

A Practical Guide to Learning a Foreign Language

Remo L. Nannetti

iUniverse, Inc.

New York Lincoln Shanghai

Mind Your Language!
A Practical Guide to Learning a Foreign Language

iUniverse, Inc.

For information address:
iUniverse, Inc.
2021 Pine Lake Road, Suite 100
Lincoln, NE 68512
www.iuniverse.com

ISBN: 0-595-31933-5

Printed in the United States of America

To my wife, Georgina, whose endless patience and infinite understanding have made this book possible.

Contents

Part IV   *Living the Language*

Foreword

You are probably reading this book because you are studying a foreign language (either on your own or through attending a class) and need some advice on making the most of your studies. You may be a committed and able student who wants to progress to a higher level, or an average student who wishes to maximise strengths and eliminate weaknesses. You might, on the other hand, be finding difficulty with some aspects of language learning. Whatever your level of ability, there are systematic ways in which you can improve your language skills. All it takes is a bit of thought, a lot of determination and a willingness to go that little step further.

Learning a language should be an enjoyable adventure, a voyage of discovery in which you visit new places and experience new sensations. If this isn't happening at the moment, then don't despair; this book will take you through a systematic evaluation of your present language learning experience and suggest ways in which it can be improved. The rest is up to you—reading this book alone will not automatically make you a better linguist, but putting the advice it gives into practice definitely will!

PART I
Helping Yourself

Explore Your Strengths and Weaknesses

There are two ways of using this book. The first way is to read it from cover to cover, making notes as you go along. The second way (and the one I recommend) is to start off by finding out a little bit about what kind of language learner you are. This chapter will take you through a checklist of what language teachers consider to be *good practice*; in other words, all the things that you, the student, can do in order to improve your knowledge and skills. Bear in mind that there are very few language learners who do absolutely everything described in the checklist. This is not surprising, as we are all individuals and learn in different ways. What might be an effective strategy with one person might turn out to be hopeless with another. What is important, though, is that we identify those areas of our learning experience in which there is room for improvement and then take positive steps to tackle them.

So let's get started. You will see below that there are fifteen main areas of language learning. Each area has nine statements of *good practice*. What you have to do is read each statement carefully and consider to what extent you do the activity described. There are three possible answers: *always, sometimes, never*. If you always do something, write the letter *A* next to the statement. If you sometimes do it, write an *S*. If the answer is never, then you've guessed it: write an *N*. (If you don't want to deface your book, then write your answers lightly in pencil.) Remember that you have to be entirely honest and truthful; it's no use deluding yourself. This is the time to reveal all, to take a long, hard but hopefully accurate look at your performance. I'll wait until you have worked your way through all 135 statements before telling you how to interpret the results. By the way, if you find that a particular statement doesn't apply to your own learning situation (e.g. the one about using the foreign language assistant) then just ignore it and go on to the next one. Ready? Let's go!

Manage Your Mind

- I am highly motivated. (13–14)
- I set myself goals and targets. (14–15)
- I am self-confident. (15–16)
- I am positive in overcoming difficulties. (16–17)
- I communicate well with others. (17–18)
- I can balance work with play. (18–19)
- I enjoy learning a foreign language. (19)
- I review my progress. (19–20)
- I reward myself when I succeed. (20)

Improve Your Learning Experience:

- I attend classes regularly and on time. (21)
- I anticipate what the teacher will be doing during the lesson. (21–22)
- I bring all the necessary materials to class. (22)
- I sit in a prominent position in class. (23)
- I volunteer answers and participate in class. (23–24)
- I am alert and attentive in class. (24)
- I ask questions during and after class. (24)
- I revise lesson notes after class. (25)
- I plan ahead to the next class. (25)

Organise Your Work:

- I note down key dates in my course of study. (28–29)

- I plan how I am going to use my time. (29–30)

- I review my use of time. (30)

- I take care over the presentation of my work. (30–31)

- I display my work prominently. (31–32)

- I use notes to remind me of things. (32)

- I file my work methodically. (32–34)

- I store my work in a convenient and accessible location. (33)

- I keep grammar and vocabulary notes. (33–34)

Listening:

- I settle myself before listening. (38)

- I make sure I can hear clearly. (38)

- I anticipate what to listen for. (39)

- I read carefully any questions I have to answer. (39)

- I listen for key words. (39)

- I concentrate fully when I listen. (39)

- I take effective notes. (40–41)

- I practise my listening skills on my own. (41–44)

- I learn vocabulary. (44)

Speaking:

- I speak at a moderate pace. (47)

- I can paraphrase when necessary. (47–48)

- I make the effort to speak. (48)

- I am not afraid of making mistakes. (49)

- I project my voice clearly. (49–50)

- I pay attention to tone, accent and pronunciation. (50–51)

- I include detail where relevant. (51–52)

- I take time to listen to the other person. (52–53)

- I actively practise my speaking skills. (54–55)

Reading:

- I consider the appearance of a text before reading it. (58–59)

- I read for the overall message before considering the detail. (59–60)

- I can read and understand the detail of a text. (60–61)

- I explore and note new constructions and vocabulary. (61–62)

- I translate from the foreign language into English. (61)

- I ask for advice on extra reading materials. (63)

- I read a variety of text types for extra practice. (65–66)

- I practise reading texts aloud. (65)

- I try to read longer and more challenging texts. (67)

Writing:

- I plan what I am going to write. (70–72)

- I write a first draft. (72–73)

- I include sufficient detail. (73–74)

- I check over what I have written. (74–77)

- I present my final draft effectively. (78)

- I do a variety of writing tasks. (79–80)

- I redraft pieces I have written previously. (80–82)

- I include my own favourite phrases and recycle material I have previously used. (82)

- I imitate good writing in others. (82–83)

Using Your Textbook:

- I take good care of my textbook. (87)

- I spend time getting to know the layout of my textbook. (88–91)

- I use the checklists in my textbook to monitor my progress. (90)

- I read ahead to the next unit or lesson. (92)

- I refer to my textbook when doing work. (92)

- I use bookmarks to mark important pages and sections. (92)

- I take notes from my textbook. (92–93)

- I use my textbook to revise. (93)

- I explore any extra resources offered by my textbook. (93)

Using a Dictionary:

- I take care over choosing a dictionary. (95–98)

- I spend time getting to know the layout of my dictionary. (99–101)

- I check the various translations of a word or expression. (100)

- I read over examples of how a word or expression is used. (100–101)

- I pay attention to notes on style and register. (101)

- I think before reaching for the dictionary. (101–102)

- I use bookmarks to mark important sections. (102–103)

- I practise using my dictionary. (103)

- I build up my word power through continuous reading. (104)

Doing Homework:

- I do all of my homework. (105–107)

- I do my homework in a suitable place. (107)

- I take breaks while doing my homework. (108)

- I look over my homework once it is corrected. (108–109)

- I redo some homework assignments. (109)

- I note down my errors. (109)

- I keep a record of my marks or grades. (109)

- I file all my pieces of homework. (109)

- I do extra homework. (109–110)

Sitting Examinations:

- I acquaint myself with the format and requirements of the examination. (113–114)

- I start to revise well before the examination. (114)

- I make up a revision plan and stick to it. (114–115)

- I practise doing past papers under test conditions. (115)

- I revise vocabulary, grammar and verbs. (115–117)

- I read over work I have done in class and at home. (117–118)

- I find a suitable place to study. (118)

- I relax the night before an examination and arrive in good time for it. (118–119)

- I consider my answers carefully, present them clearly and leave enough time for checking. (119–120)

Using Computers:

- I word-process my work. (126–127)

- I store my work on the computer. (127)

- I keep paper copies of my computer-based materials. (127)

- I use language-learning software. (128)

- I evaluate language-learning software before using it. (128–129)

- I use the Internet to help me with my language learning. (130–132)

- I e-mail pen-friends in the foreign language. (132–133)

- I e-mail my teacher. (133–134)

- I use voice messaging, text chat and voice chat. (134–135)

Sound and Vision:

- I watch foreign language broadcasts on live television. (137–138)

- I use the audio-visual facilities in my place of learning. (137)

- I watch foreign language films and programmes on video, DVD and at the cinema. (139–140)

- I exploit the soundtrack and subtitling possibilities of DVD. (140)

- I listen to foreign language broadcasts on radio. (140–141)

- I borrow audio-visual materials from my place of learning or local library. (141–142)

- I access the audio-visual materials linked to my textbook. (142)

- I listen to songs and poetry in the foreign language. (142–143)

- I listen to spoken books in the foreign language. (142)

People Power:

- I ask my teacher for help and advice. (145)

- I enquire about my progress. (145)

- I collaborate with my fellow students. (145–146)

- I share my learning experiences with my fellow students. (147)

- I involve members of my family in my language learning. (147–148)

- I update my family on my progress. (148–149)

- I work with the foreign language assistant. (149–150)

- I have access to a foreign language tutor. (150–151)

- I take extra classes. (151)

Getting Abroad:

- I go on holiday to the country whose language I am studying. (153)

- I go on trips organised by my place of learning to the country whose language I am studying. (153–154)

- I take part in exchanges organised by my place of learning to the country whose language I am studying. (154–155)

- I attend language courses abroad. (155)

- I do work experience or voluntary service abroad. (155–156)

- I talk to as many people as possible while abroad. (157)

- I follow the local way of life while abroad. (157–158)

- I note down things I learn while abroad. (158)

- I access the local media while abroad. (158)

OK, so you've worked your way through all the statements. (This is quite an achievement in itself, given there are so many!) It's now time to have a closer look at the answers you gave. At this point you might be thinking that this is going to be like one of those magazine quizzes where you award each answer a certain number of points, calculate your total and read a description of how you've done. No: what I want you to do is much simpler, and there are two ways of doing it. The first way assumes that you don't mind marking your book; if this is the case, take two highlighters of different colours and highlight all the statements against which you wrote an *S* and an *N* (remember that *S* means that you *sometimes* do this and *N* that you *never* do it). Use a different colour for both types of answer so that you can easily tell them apart. The second way involves taking two sheets of paper. Write this heading at the top of the first sheet: *Things I sometimes do.* On the top of the second sheet write *Things I never do.* Now go over your answers and make up two lists, remembering to copy out the page references printed next to each statement.

You now have a summary of those areas of your language learning in which you could improve. What you now have to do is prioritise: in other words, decide which areas require your immediate attention. Obviously these will all be on the list of things you *never* do. There will be other things that are not immediate priorities because you are already doing them to a limited extent (i.e. your *sometimes* list). Start by identifying five things on your *never* list that you think you can undertake. Now read the corresponding sections in the book (see the page references at the end of each of the statements you have worked your way through). Then comes the crucial part—starting to do what you perhaps have never tried before, or felt afraid about doing. This is the bit that is up to you; after all, it's no use reading this book and not acting on any of the advice it gives! Remember to remain positive; we can all improve if we have the will to do so.

Once you have dealt with the first five things on your *never* list, continue with the others until you get to the end of the list. Then start in the same way on your *sometimes* list. It will take time, but you will get there. Be methodical and determined, and remain positive and adventurous at all times. Remember that people will always be there to help you should you need assistance or encouragement; all you have to do is ask! A final word: when it's all getting on top of you, think of this proverb: *Perseverance is not a long race; it is many short races one after another.*

In other words, take things one at a time, and if you keep doing this the big picture will take care of itself.

Manage Your Mind

Learning a language is all in the mind. This does not mean that you have to be exceptionally intelligent in order to learn a language. Obviously it does help if you have some natural ability and brainpower, but these things in themselves are not an automatic guarantee of success. What is much more important is your mental attitude; in other words, the way in which you approach the whole business of language learning. I like to call it *managing your mind*; after all, the mind is a large and complex thing, and we have to learn how to exert some order and control over it. This sounds difficult, but there are some simple steps that we can take to make sure that our minds are in peak condition for language learning.

Motivate Yourself!

The first step is to *motivate* yourself. Start by asking yourself why you want to learn a foreign language. It may be because a foreign language will be useful to you in your chosen career, or because you want to live and work in a foreign country. Alternatively, your only reason for learning a foreign language might be that you enjoy it and find it of interest. Whatever the reasons might be, you have to be clear in your mind about them.

Why not write them all out on a large sheet of paper? Put as your heading *Why do I want to learn a foreign language?* and then list your own personal reasons for doing so. You may find that the reasons you put down are basically your own ambitions. How do you achieve them? A big question, and one that doesn't have a simple answer. How desperately do you want to achieve them? You'll find this easier to answer. Basically, the more you want to do something, the less you have to motivate yourself in order to do it. If your lifelong and heartfelt ambition is to become a languages teacher, then you will devote all your energies to your language studies. Nobody will need to encourage you to work hard; you will have a burning desire to succeed in your chosen path, and you will be highly motivated in every aspect of your work.

But wait a minute—not all of us are like that! Perhaps we're only studying a language because we have to, and have no great love for language learning. We may be the kind of student who is continually reprimanded by teachers and parents for not trying hard enough. But at the end of the day we still have to get through the course, and we can only do that by motivating ourselves sufficiently. There is a well-known saying that goes something like this: *Nothing succeeds like success.* Success in our studies improves our motivation; in other words, if we feel we have succeeded in one aspect of our language learning then we are spurred on to do even better in the next. Success breeds confidence, and confidence in turn improve motivation. But how do we get there? The best way is to set ourselves *targets* and then overtake them.

Set Yourself Targets

If you have worked your way through the previous chapter you should have a good idea of the various areas in which you can improve. As I said in that chapter, it's a good idea to start off with about five things that you are definitely *not* doing at the moment. Then consider how you are going to tackle them, and how long it is going to take you. If you write this all on a sheet of paper it should look something like this:

MY BIG FIVE LANGUAGE-LEARNING TARGETS

- *I am going to do all my assignments.*

- *I am going to take more care over the presentation of my work.*

- *I am going to volunteer more answers in class.*

- *I am going to practise listening skills on my own.*

- *I am going to ask my teacher for advice much more often.*

I AM GOING TO TRY TO DO ALL THIS BY CHRISTMAS!

What you now have to do is to remind yourself constantly of your targets. It's no use making up your list and then forgetting all about it! (After all, you don't want this to resemble the average New Year's resolution that usually only last a few days.) There are several ways of doing this. One of the best is to display copies of your targets all around you, where you can see them clearly and be continuously reminded of them. Possible places might be on the walls of your room, on the headboard of your bed, on the refrigerator door, in the front page of your diary, on the cover of your exercise book or notebook, or even as wallpaper on your computer screen; it doesn't matter where it is, as long as you can see it, again and again and again! With a bit of luck these constant reminders will be highly effective and you will have no excuses for not attempting to overtake your targets.

Get Working

Now it's crunch time. You've worked on your motivation and established your targets. The next step is to achieve those targets. Once again your mental attitude is vital to your success. Research has shown that effective language learners possess certain key qualities:

• They are self-confident.

• They are positive in overcoming difficulties.

• They can communicate effectively with others.

• They enjoy what they are doing.

Let's take some time to look at each of these in greater detail.

Build Up Your Self-Confidence

Building up your self-confidence is vital to your success as a language learner. One of the main problems I encounter as a teacher concerns those students who have good ability but lack self-belief. They constantly tell themselves that something is going to be very difficult and that they will probably not be able to do it; they don't want to take chances and always prefer to play it safe; they have a low opinion of their abilities and refuse to believe that they can improve; in short, they are afraid.

Afraid of what? Usually it's fear of failing, fear of letting themselves and other people down, fear of humiliating themselves in front of their fellow students. The result is that they form a defence mechanism that involves retreating into their shell and only emerging when they are totally sure of achieving success. One of my colleagues has described this as remaining in the *comfort zone*. What is a *comfort zone*? It's what I have just described; a pattern of behaviour that involves keeping a low profile, taking no risks whatsoever, avoiding possible embarrassing situations, and refusing to take the initiative. Students who remain in the *comfort zone* will usually get through their work, but they will seldom excel in it, simply because they are not prepared to push the boat out and sail in uncharted waters.

Obviously if you want to do really well in your language studies then you have to abandon the *comfort zone* and start living dangerously. For example, if your teacher asks a question and you are only half-sure of the answer, don't sit back and play it safe by not putting up your hand; get out of your *comfort zone* and go for it. It's no big deal if you get it wrong; in fact, the important thing is to learn from your mistakes and not be afraid of making them. (The Italians have a good proverb about mistakes: *Sbagliando, si impara,* i.e. you learn by making mistakes.)

But remember that you might get that question right. If you do, you will feel really good about yourself and you will have built up a little more self-confidence. Another proverb springs to mind (not Italian, this time): *Nothing ventured, nothing gained.* So tell yourself you are going to take the initiative and do things instead of letting fear of failure ruin your chances.

Be Positive in Overcoming Difficulty

It would be wrong of me to say that learning a language is easy. No matter how good a student you are, you are going to encounter problems along the way. Some students find difficulty in speaking the language, others in listening to it; many struggle with writing the language accurately while others cannot grasp a particular grammatical point.

If you did the review at the beginning of the book you will have a clear idea of the particular areas where you yourself encounter difficulty. The important thing, however, is to realise that this is a totally natural occurrence in all language learning; we all meet with difficulties from time to time, and it is vital that we deal with them in a positive fashion.

Let's go back to the statement we made at the beginning of the chapter: *Learning a language is all in the mind.* Most of the difficulties we encounter in learning a foreign language can be minimised by making sure that we remain in a positive frame of mind. Here are some pieces of advice that you may find useful:

- First of all, don't panic! There are very few problems that cannot be solved in this world. Stay calm; take a deep breath, compose yourself and say to yourself: *I can do this. This is not a problem. This is a difficulty thousands of other people have had. They got over it; I am going to get over it as well. It's only difficult if I think it's difficult. I'm now going to take the first step towards doing something about it.*

- Ask yourself what you can do to deal with the difficulty. Perhaps you're tired and your brain isn't functioning as well as it normally does; in that case, walk away! Take a break, get some rest and then come back to the problem with a refreshed mind. Often you'll find that what seemed difficult before is now much easier to cope with.

- Remember that we all need help from time to time. Don't be afraid or ashamed to ask for it. Many difficulties can be resolved if we ask someone else to help us. But you have to make that first move; it's no use suffering in silence, as the difficulty you are having will not go away of its own accord. In language learning, you have to make things happen. Teachers are not mind readers; often they will not know you have a problem unless you make the effort to tell them. Getting help with something you find difficult is far better than struggling in silence trying to crack it on your own!

- Finally, learn from your experience of dealing with difficulty. Once you overcome a difficulty, think about the steps you took to resolve it, taking time to list these in the precise order in which they occurred. Then if something similar happens in future, you'll know exactly how to cope with it. It's all about self-confidence; if you believe with all your heart that you can resolve a difficulty, then the chances are that you probably will. The greater your self-confidence, the easier it is to sail effortlessly through any obstacle laid in your path.

Learn to Communicate with Other People

You may have heard an advertising slogan for a telephone company telling us that *It's good to talk.* Obviously what they are trying to do is convince us all to make more phone calls, but the same slogan could definitely be applied to language learning. I'm not talking here about the need to practise speaking a foreign language (we'll deal with this in a future chapter); what I mean is that we have to *speak and communicate with those people involved in our language learning.* In other words, we have to keep them informed about how well we are doing, what difficulties we are having, what we think of the course, how we think we can improve, etc. Who are these people? They are not only teachers, but also our family members and fellow students.

At this point, I would like to say that the thing that frustrates me most about many students is that they don't talk to me! Perhaps that's my fault, but I always try to be pleasant, helpful and approachable, so I don't think that's the problem. As I said earlier, teachers are not mind readers; we normally have a good idea of your ability and the progress you have made, but there will often be things that we don't know and that we would like you to share with us. There is a name for this: it's called *feedback*. So remember to keep talking to your teacher; the more he or she knows about your language learning experience, the better. It's *good to talk*, and not only in the foreign language!

Finally, remember what I said earlier; don't just talk to your teacher, but involve your family and fellow students in your language learning. Talk about what you're doing, how you're getting on, where you want to go with your language. Bear in mind that we are all part of a *learning community*, and that to be an effective member of that community we have to communicate clearly, constantly, and confidently.

Enjoy What You Are Doing

In this chapter we have been talking about managing your mind so that you can study a foreign language more effectively. All serious stuff! However, you may be surprised to learn that being *too* serious can actually be counterproductive. Like everything in life, you have to take things in moderation.

It's no use studying every free moment of the day or for long, uninterrupted periods of time without ever taking a break. The brain is like any other part of the body: it can get tired. A tired brain means that you will not learn as much, and what you learn may soon be forgotten. Research has shown that reasonably short, concentrated spells of language learning are much more effective than long hours spent poring over books. So be sensible—don't overtax yourself. You have to learn to balance work with play. As the proverb says, *All work and no play makes Jack a dull boy*. If Jack had been learning a foreign language then he probably wouldn't have progressed very far.

One last thing to remember—learning a foreign language should be fun. Ideally we should all enjoy the process, but often this doesn't happen. Whatever the reason, however, you have to ensure that you remain positive at all times. If you approach things in the right frame of mind, then you will find that you enjoy doing them. It's all about our attitude; students who take a negative attitude to their language learning are automatically ruling out any possibility of enjoying what they will be doing.

You have to keep smiling however difficult the task might seem; if you're successful, then you will start to enjoy what you are doing, and who knows, even if you are unsuccessful then you might still be enjoying it! (I don't mean by this that we should enjoy making mistakes; but remember that you can always turn the process of making a mistake into a positive experience by reacting to it with humour and understanding.)

A happy learner is an effective learner; if you enjoy your work and adopt a relaxed yet methodical approach to it, then you will rapidly build up your confidence and progress to greater things. So believe in yourself and your own abilities, and look forward to every challenge with a smile on your face.

Review and Reward

So you have taken the advice I've given you so far. You have explored your strengths and weaknesses and you have worked on your self-motivation. You have set yourself targets. In achieving your targets you have built up your self-confidence and have overcome difficulties along the way. You have communicated effectively with others and have actively enjoyed what you have been doing. What now, you may ask. The answer is simple. You now have to review your progress and reward yourself if you have been successful.

Let's start with the review. How do you know you have been successful in achieving your targets? Here are some ways in which progress might show itself:

• You may be achieving better marks or grades.

• Your teacher may be praising you more often.

• You may feel more confident when faced with language-learning situations.

Sometimes it's difficult to assess how effectively we have achieved a target, but don't worry; the very fact that you are reviewing your progress is a positive step in the right direction. The best thing to do if you feel uncomfortable with the whole process of self-assessment is to ask your teacher to do it for you (or even someone else who is acquainted with your language learning, such as one of your fellow students). They will be able to comment on your progress as long as you explain to them the areas in which you have been trying to improve (the best time to do this is, of course, just after you have decided on your targets and are about to start trying to overtake them; that way, they will know what to look for and will feel more confident about giving you an opinion).

Finally, learn to reward yourself. Or better still, get someone else to reward you! Here's one idea that can be very effective and motivating: when you are writing out your targets, include the reward that will be yours if you achieve them. Here's an example that also involves a time-scale:

I am going to volunteer more answers in class starting from tomorrow until the end of the month, when I shall ask my teacher if he has seen any difference. If he has, then I'm going to buy myself a new CD player.

If you are relying on other people to reward you, then remember that it's only polite to check it out with them first!

The Final Word

Let's list the various things I have suggested you do:

- Motivate yourself.

- Set yourself targets.

- Become more self-confident.

- Be positive in overcoming difficulties.

- Communicate effectively with others.

- Enjoy what you are doing.

- Review your progress.

- Reward yourself.

What are you waiting for? Get to it!

Improve Your Learning Experience

The environment in which we learn a language is vitally important. The best one of all is being in the foreign country, but for many of us this is not always possible. It may be that you are attempting to learn a language all on your own, but the chances are that you are part of a class being taught by a teacher at your local place of learning. If this is the case, then you are part of what is often called a *learning community*, made up of your teacher, your fellow students, other teachers and students, managers, and possibly parents and family.

Your experience of learning a foreign language is therefore limited for the most part to what you learn within the four walls of a classroom. That is not to say that we cannot learn elsewhere; on the contrary, much effective language learning can and does take place away from the teacher. However, most of what you know about the language you are learning will have been taught to you traditionally by a teacher within a classroom.

Faced with this particular scenario, we have to learn to maximise our classroom experiences, to get the most out of the limited time we can spend in the company of our teacher and fellow students. This chapter will suggest a variety of ways in which this can be achieved.

Before the Class

Improving your learning experience starts before you even arrive at class. If you are starting the class for the first time, make sure you know all the basics: when it is, where it is and how you get there. Unfortunately first impressions are often lasting ones, and turning up late at your first class with a new teacher is not the greatest way of getting noticed. Once the classes get under way, make sure that you always arrive punctually, with a few moments to spare before the start. This will give you time to sit down, take out your materials and compose yourself before the teacher begins the lesson.

At this point I'd like to mention that you should try to attend classes as regularly as possible; if you often miss them then you are making it very difficult to achieve any consistency in your learning. The more it happens, the worse it is, as you will begin to fall behind. Catching up on missed work is always more difficult than doing the work when you are first given it. Asking your fellow students to help you out also inconveniences their learning experience. So the best policy is the simplest one—be there!

A few other things to mention before you arrive at class. The first is about anticipating what the teacher is going to be doing. Sometimes you will know what is going to be happening because the teacher will have told you during the previous lesson. Other times, you will have to think about what might happen. Often this isn't too difficult because teachers are very much creatures of habit and tend to follow set patterns of behaviour. In any case, you should get into the habit of thinking about the next lesson. Ask yourself these questions:

- *Where did the teacher stop last day?*

- *Have I looked over my lesson notes for my last class?*

- *Have I done the homework for my last class?*

- *What is going to happen in the next class?*

- *Is there any way I can read or prepare ahead so that I'll have a better idea of what the teacher will be doing?*

The next thing is a basic one, but very important nevertheless. Remember to bring all the materials you're going to need: pens, stationery, textbook, notebook, exercise books, homework, etc. As a practising teacher I know only too well how frustrating and time-wasting it can be when my students arrive at class without one or more things needed for the lesson. They inconvenience themselves and others and get the lesson off to a bad start. More importantly, the quality of their own learning experience suffers as they struggle to get through the lesson without a vital piece of equipment.

Remember that organisation and thoughtfulness pay dividends, as you will arrive at your class ready to make the most of it. Bear in mind that the time put into preparing for a class can sometimes be as valuable as the time spent in it.

During the Class

You've done the difficult bit—you've made it on time and brought the necessary materials. What's more, you are mentally prepared for the lesson ahead. What we are now going to look at are ways in which you can maximise your classroom experience.

The first important thing is where you sit in the classroom. Some teachers have a seating plan that you have to stick to, while others don't mind where you sit. If you are in a position to decide where to sit, consider the following points:

- Always sit in a prominent position, where the teacher can see you clearly.

- Sit where you can see the board properly.

- Sit beside students with whom you feel comfortable working (not necessarily your friends, as these might prove to be a distraction!).

- Don't change your seat from class to class.

If the teacher has his or her prearranged seating plan, then you may have no choice in the matter. Many teachers take great care over their seating plans to ensure that classes are split into ability or behavioural groups. In other words, there is a precise and logical reason why your teacher has asked you to sit in a particular position. If this is the case, then trust his or her judgement. If you feel you need a change (for example, you may be seated near students who distract you from your work) then ask your teacher to re-seat you. The important thing is that you sit in a position where you can follow the work of the class effectively and work easily with those students around you.

The next thing I'm going to talk about is by far the most important of all. It concerns the way you act in class, the way in which you interact with the teacher and lesson. Learning a foreign language is an active process; in other words, you have to take the initiative, push yourself forward and make sure you are getting the maximum out of your learning experience. You can do this in the following ways:

- **Volunteer your answers.** Students are often reluctant to give answers because they are afraid they may be wrong. You have to banish this thought from your head when you learn a language! Remember that it's much better to give an incorrect answer than no answer at all. Even a guess is better than silence. As one of my colleagues says, the best students are always the most willing guessers. One of the most frustrating things I find as a languages teacher is the situation where I ask a question and nobody volunteers a response. However, when I ask a student the same question directly I then discover that they know the correct answer! I think what happens is that many students in class prefer to stay in their own *comfort zone* (remember that we talked about this in the previous chapter). They feel relaxed and unchallenged sitting quietly in class, letting things happen around them and never making the effort to become part of the teaching and learning process. They are attentive and hard working, but don't want to be thrust into the spotlight. Sometimes it's a question of character; quiet, shy people will never want to push themselves forward. But when you're learning a language, forwardness pays off, so if you're one of those shy, retiring types, step out of the *comfort zone* and into the limelight.

- **Be alert and attentive at all times.** Don't be distracted by other students sitting near you. Focus exclusively on the teacher and the lesson. Keep reminding yourself why you are in the class: not to chat with friends, not to daydream, not to misbehave, but to learn a language. If you have worked on your motivation and have targets to achieve then this will not be difficult. Your own energy level is also important; it goes without saying that a good night's sleep is vital if you are to remain alert for long periods. Don't forget that the brain needs nourishment and fresh air if it is to function effectively, so have a good breakfast, don't skip lunch, drink plenty fluids throughout the day and don't always stay indoors. That way when you enter the languages classroom you will have no problem keeping up your concentration.

- **Ask plenty questions.** Sometimes a teacher will explain something that you don't fully understand. It's all too easy just to let it slip by and do nothing about it. The smart languages student asks the teacher either straightaway or at a convenient point in the lesson. That way they get a firm response from the teacher that should clear up the difficulty. Good teachers encourage their students to ask questions; it's all part of the learning process and provides teachers with instant feedback on how effective (or not!) their teaching has been.

- **Participate in your language learning.** If the teacher asks for a volunteer to do something active in the foreign language, then push yourself forward and say that you'll do it. Remember that you can only improve in a language by constantly launching yourself into more and more challenging learning situations. The initiative has to come from you; you have to live dangerously, try out new things, and put yourself in full view of your fellow students. Who knows, you might end up inspiring them to join in! Try to be a leader in class; stop thinking about what others might think, dismiss from your mind any doubts or difficulties that might arise, and make the teacher notice you.

After the Class

The class has now finished and guess what—there are still a few things you should be doing! Students often think that just because a lesson has come to an end they can forget all about it. This is not the case; effective language learning involves following up all of your lessons in a consistent and methodical way, so that you don't let what you have learned slip away. Here are a few things that you should try to do:

- **Clear up difficulties.** Sometimes there will be something you didn't understand during the lesson but didn't get a chance to ask about. If this happens, try to ask the teacher about it once the lesson has ended. As I have said before, teachers like students who communicate with them. Many problems can be easily dealt with at the end of lessons; if the teacher is in a hurry or if the problem requires extensive explanation, then they will probably arrange to give you help some other time.

- **Read over your notes.** Look over your notes later on in the day, while the lesson is still relatively fresh in your mind. Think about the different phases of the lesson, and how the teacher presented them. Ask yourself what you have learnt, and how you are going to make use of it in the future.

- **Think forward to the next lesson.** The chances are that the teacher will be building on what you have done in the previous lesson, so make sure that you have understood all of it. Often we think we have understood everything in class, only to find out when we look over our notes that it isn't quite as simple as we first thought. In that case check it out with your teacher before the next lesson comes along.

- **Continue working at home.** Make sure you do any homework the teacher has given you as soon as possible after the class; that way you won't have forgotten any advice or information the teacher gave you, and it will still be fresh in your mind. If the teacher didn't give you any homework, then invent some. I don't need to tell you that doing extra work is seriously good for your foreign language learning!

The Final Word

All the advice I have given you in this chapter can be neatly summed up in one word: **PAPER**. Students who *paper* each class they attend are well on the way to success in learning a foreign language:

Prepare, Anticipate, Participate, Enquire, Review

- **Before** the class **prepare** properly and try to **anticipate** what the teacher will be doing.

- **During** the class **participate** actively and **enquire** about what you are doing.

- **After** the class **review** what you have done.

If you do this consistently with every class you attend then you will maximise your learning experience. Teachers will tell you that learning doesn't just happen; it needs some input from you, the student. So make the most of your time in class; nobody else (not even a teacher) can do this, it's totally up to you!

Organise Your Work

Good organisation is the key to effective learning. Students who are well-organised find the whole learning process much more straightforward, and are more likely to succeed. Why is this the case? If you think about this for a moment you will probably come up with the following reasons:

- Good organisation saves time.

- Good organisation saves energy.

- Good organisation makes a positive impression on others.

- Good organisation makes it easier to learn.

How does this relate to learning a foreign language? The first thing to consider is that the process of learning a language depends on many things: your own natural ability, your self-motivation, your self-confidence, the time you have available, the opportunities you have to practise, and so on. However all these things are made very much more difficult if you lack good organisational skills.

Effective organisation is the key to getting things done quickly, easily and efficiently. Obviously some of us are better at this than others; we all know people who are incredibly well-organised and whose entire lives are conducted with military precision, and we tend to admire them. Then there are the other disorganised beings amongst us who exist in a state of confusion and chaos, and who either fill us with pity or drive us to distraction. Which category do you come into? Most people are somewhere in the middle, so there is always room for improvement.

How can good organisation help you to learn a foreign language? There are four main areas I would like you to consider:

- Forward planning.

- Time management.

- Presentation of work.

- Storage.

Let's look at each of these in greater detail.

Forward Planning

This is all about looking ahead and trying to anticipate what you're going to be doing in the course of your studies. How far ahead should you look? The answer to this is simple: as far as possible! For most students this will be the academic year, which will normally be divided into terms or semesters. The first step is to get a diary or some kind of personal organiser into which you can enter all your data. Do this at the very beginning of the academic year and enter the following dates:

- When terms or semesters begin and end.

- Holidays.

- Class tests and assessments.

- Formal examinations.

- Homework and assignment deadlines.

- Start and finish times of particular units of work.

Once you do this, you will have an overview of the entire year that will be useful for planning ahead. At first it may be difficult to get all this information, but your teachers should be able to help you with most of it. The important thing is to remember to enter all new important dates in your diary or organiser as soon as you learn of them. It also helps if you use highlighters to differentiate your entries; for example, you could highlight all the dates of your speaking assessments in yellow and your homework completion dates in green. That way when you look at a full week or month you can see at a glance what is coming up.

The next thing to do is make sure that you have listed your targets in a prominent position in your diary or organiser. (These are the targets that we talked about in *Managing Your Mind*.) By this I mean a place where you will constantly see and be reminded of them. If you have set yourself a time-scale for each target, then make sure you have entered the dates in your calendar.

Finally, remember that forward planning only works if you take the time to check at what point you are at and where you will be going. Let me put this another way; it is no use spending a lot of time entering dates and targets into a diary or personal organiser if you don't look at it on a daily basis. Once you get into the habit of doing this, you'll find that you can cope better with your workload.

Time Management

Time is precious. Think of it; you only get so many hours and minutes of language tuition from your teachers. The last chapter was all about using that time effectively, so that you get the maximum benefit from your language lessons. But as we know, language learning doesn't stop there; it should continue outside the classroom, and this is where students get into difficulty. How much extra time should you devote to your language studies? How can you plan and manage this time effectively? Time management techniques can help you to make these decisions and stick to them. Here are a few pieces of advice:

- **Consider the big picture.** Look at your commitments and responsibilities not only for languages, but also for other subjects you may be studying.

- **Quantify your time.** Decide how much extra time you can spend each night at home on your language studies. It could be a half-hour, an hour or even more. If necessary, get advice from your teacher.

- **Identify available time.** Try to choose a regular time-slot each night. For example, you could decide that from seven to eight o'clock is languages time. Once you have decided this, make sure your family know about it so that they can remind you to get back to work if they spot you watching television!

- **Stick to your plan.** If you have decided to spend an hour each night on your language studies, then do exactly that. Don't be tempted to go over your time. It is better to do a regular, fixed amount each night of the week rather than a big block of work lasting several hours on one night only. Languages benefit more than any other subject from regular practice.

- **Plan ahead.** Have a clear idea in your head about what you are going to do during your extra time. For example, decide earlier in the day that you are going to spend that evening's language study time looking over your vocabulary or reading over your grammar notes. If you don't know what you are going to do at the moment you sit down to do it, then you will inevitably waste a lot of time trying to figure out what to do. Common sense, really!

- **Log your time.** Enter the hours you have done each day in your diary or personal organiser. Then count up the hours you do each week or month. That way you will feel a sense of achievement and you can set targets for yourself. The good thing about reaching your targets is that you then have a good excuse for rewarding yourself!

Presentation of Work

At regular intervals during your study of a foreign language your teacher will give you assignments or homework exercises. Sometimes these involve what we language teachers call *learning* work; in other words, learning things off by heart, such as new vocabulary and grammar constructions. Other times you will be given speaking assignments, such as preparing for a short speech, presentation or extended conversation in the foreign language. However, much of your work will be in written form: doing grammar exercises, writing out new vocabulary, writing essays, and doing translations. This is where presentation is important. Teachers will tell you that even the best of essays can lose marks if it is presented untidily. What do they mean?

- Handwriting that is difficult to make out.

- Words and sentences messily scored out.

- Additions squeezed in between lines.

- Pen colours that are difficult to read.

- Footnotes and afterthoughts written in the margin or after the main text.

- Poor quality paper.

- Stains, creases and tears.

Nowadays many students prefer to word-process their work rather than write it out by hand. This is a perfectly acceptable solution and is welcomed by most teachers. The advantages are obvious: your work is much easier to read, you can add and delete words or sections of text before printing out, and you can store your work on computer, ready to be redrafted or added to on a future occasion. However, there are a few things you have to watch out for:

- Make sure your typing skills are adequate. If they are not, then you will end up making a lot of spelling mistakes that would not occur if you wrote the text by hand.

- Learn how to insert accents on the computer; adding them in by hand afterwards doesn't look great and you always tend to miss out a few.

- Avoid unusual fonts and strange colours.

- Use double-spacing; it looks much neater and the teacher will have room to write in comments.

- Keep back-ups of all work you store on the computer.

If you feel unsure about word processing (or are one of those people who are uncomfortable with computers) then write out your work by hand. Remember that it is the quality of what you write that is important; just because something is beautifully word-processed does not necessarily mean that it is a great piece of work.

If you do decide to write out your work by hand then take care that your handwriting is neat, tidy and legible. (I once had a tutor who told me that messy handwriting was often a sign of genius, but many years in the classroom have convinced me otherwise!) Once again I recommend that you go for double-spacing, using correction fluid if you make a mistake (a word of caution: many students paint over errors with correction fluid only to forget to write in the correction once it has dried). Try to use a good-quality pen that doesn't smudge and once again avoid strange colours; nothing is worse than trying to read something written in bright pink fluorescent ink! Red is a colour that you should also avoid as many teachers tend to correct work with a red pen.

Finally, regardless of whether you word-process or hand-write your work, use good quality paper. Longer essays or assignments also look better if they are presented in plastic folders or polythene pockets. First impressions are often lasting impressions, and if you make the teacher's life easier by handing in a nicely presented piece of work, then you may be halfway to getting that great grade you dream of!

So far I have talked about how you present written work to your teacher. Let's now talk about what you can do when you get your work back. Imagine you've done a good piece of work; a great essay in the foreign language full of super phrases, distinctive vocabulary, and well presented into the bargain. Ask yourself what you do with it. Many students will file it away, so that it remains hidden from view, buried under a pile of other papers or lost at the back of a drawer. This is not a good idea; as the proverb says, *Out of sight, out of mind.*

It is much better to display your work in prominent positions so that you can be constantly reminded of it. You could, for example, have a languages notice board in your room, where you can pin up important pieces of work for yourself and other family members to see. You can also use the board as a place to post all those sticky notes reminding you of things you have to do for your languages classes. If you don't have space for a board then try the wall (watch you don't damage the wallpaper) or even the refrigerator, where you can use fridge-magnets to hold your work in place. Don't forget that you may be able to display your work at your place of learning; many languages departments have a notice board for students' work. The important thing about displaying your work in this way is that you have a constant visual reminder of it, which is good for learning purposes. It also raises other people's awareness of your interest and progress in your language studies and gives you, the student, a feeling of pride and achievement.

Let's return for a moment to the point that displaying work can help you to learn. It should be remembered that this is also a highly effective way of learning vocabulary. For example, if you have been asked to revise house and home vocabulary then why not label all your household objects in the foreign language? That way you will learn and retain vocabulary every time you move through the house. Other vocabulary topics can be done by devising bilingual wall charts (foreign language on one side, English on the other) and posting these in strategic places all around you. (If you are good at art you can replace the English with drawings or sketches.) One student I know had the bright idea of typing up vocabulary lists on her computer and then displaying them as desktop wallpaper. That way, every time she sat and looked at her computer desktop her vocabulary was staring at her in the face! Once she felt she knew it she would then change the wallpaper to a new vocabulary topic. By the end of the year she was achieving full marks in vocabulary tests!

Storage

During the time you spend studying a foreign language you will accumulate a lot of different materials for which you will be responsible. Here are some of the things I'm talking about:

- Textbooks and dictionaries.

- Exercise books and notebooks.

- Class handouts.

- Written work and notes done on loose-leaf paper.

- Assessment, test and examination scripts.

- Cassettes and CD's.

It is vital that you devise an efficient system of storing all these materials. By *efficient* I mean a system that is fast and simple to operate, is reasonably light and portable and takes up minimal space. It also has to be located in a convenient spot where it can be retrieved at a moment's notice. (Even the best filing system in the world is useless if you can't get at it!) This is especially important if you don't have a fixed place (such as a desk at home) from which you can study, and you have to move about from place to place.

Obviously there are many different ways of filing and storing your languages materials. Some students put everything in a box; others set aside a particular part of their bag; many use a plastic carrier. None of these solutions is particularly effective. What I recommend is that you purchase what is known as a *lever-arch file*. This is like a ring-binder but with the essential difference that the posts are quite tall and can store many more pages. There is also an adjustable clamp that keeps the pages firmly together. Then get some plastic pockets and some dividers; these will allow you to organise your file into different sections. One possible layout is given below:

- **DIARY or YEAR PLANNER:** this could be placed at the beginning of the file rather than carry it separately.

- **MY TARGETS:** the language learning targets you have set yourself, with possible time-scales and rewards.

- **CLASSWORK:** different pieces of work you have done in class; notes you have taken; exercise books (old and current).

- **GRAMMAR:** your own grammar notes, including sheets and handouts issued by your teacher; any grammar exercises you have done.

- **VOCABULARY:** vocabulary you have noted down yourself (possibly arranged into different topic areas); vocabulary sheets issued by your teacher.

- **HOMEWORK:** completed homework tasks already corrected by the teacher; homework to be handed in.

- **ASSESSMENT:** completed assessments and tests already corrected by the teacher.

- **MISCELLANEOUS:** bits and pieces, e.g. floppy disks, CD's, folders, booklets, textbooks (if not too large).

File everything in plastic pockets; this keeps it all clean and you don't have to use reinforcers to stop the pages from tearing out. (You can also get zipped pockets for storing the items listed under *Miscellaneous*.) Once you have everything organised it'll be much easier and quicker to find what you're looking for. You'll be able to start work immediately; no more wasting time looking for different things in different places. Devising an efficient storage system can take a lot of effort, but once you have done it the time savings can be quite considerable.

The Final Word

If there is one thing you should have learnt from this chapter, it is that good organisation is vital if you are to succeed in your study of a foreign language. Remember the four areas we talked about: *forward planning, time management, presentation of work, storage*. This can all be summed up in a simple rhyme:

> *Plan ahead and time beware,*
> *Present and store with care.*

Or, in the words of the poet John Dryden (1631–1700):

> *Set all things in their own peculiar place,*
> *And know that order is the greatest grace.*

So get organised—you know it makes sense!

PART II
Practice Makes Perfect

Listening

If you ask most language students which skill they find the trickiest, many will reply that they often find it difficult to listen effectively. There is something about the art of listening that fills us with apprehension, especially when we are told that we have to listen to a text or conversation in a foreign language (often spoken by native speakers) and either report back on what it all means or answer specific questions on its content. Immediately all sorts of questions begin to race through our mind: how fast will they be talking? Will I get a chance to hear it again? Will I know all the vocabulary? As a result we feel under stress before we even start to listen (some of us, of course, can deal with this better than others).

Not all listening in a foreign language is stressful, of course, but it is true to say that effective listeners are those who have the ability to concentrate on what is being said and react appropriately to it. We can all do this; it's just that some of us need more practice than others. Good listening techniques have to be worked at, and the purpose of this chapter is to teach you how to listen effectively whatever the situation in which you find yourself.

Types of Listening

Mastering a foreign language involves practising your listening skills in a variety of different situations. These can be split into two broad categories:

- **Formal listening**: you have been told what to listen for and may hear the material once or several times.

- **Informal listening**: you listen to get the overall meaning and only hear the material once.

Here are some examples of *formal listening* that you might come across in a foreign language class:

- Listening to a recorded passage or dialogue played by the teacher once or several times and answering questions on it.

- Listening to sections of a tape or CD and replaying them as often as you need to for comprehension.

- Listening to another person talk to you and asking them to repeat things you don't understand.

Informal listening can include the following:

- Listening to a radio or television programme for enjoyment.

- Listening to other people talk amongst themselves.

- Listening to someone make a speech.

It doesn't really matter which of these situations you find yourself in; to listen effectively you have to adopt the correct technique. Here is one approach that many of my students have found useful.

The Five Steps to Effective Listening

The first step is to **SETTLE YOURSELF**. In formal listening the fact that you may have to answer precise questions about something you have never heard before can make even the calmest amongst us panic. All sorts of thoughts go through our mind: what if there are words I can't understand? What if I cannot hear the text clearly? What if it's too fast for me? The trick is to dismiss all this negative thinking from your mind. Think positive; be confident in your own ability to listen effectively; tell yourself that increased self-confidence reduces the level of panic. Be relaxed, but at the same time alert and focused on the task in hand.

If you can, ask the teacher for a sound check before the exercise begins; knowing that you can hear clearly will get you off to the best possible start. If you can't hear clearly, then ask the teacher if the volume can be raised—if it cannot then try to sit closer to the sound source. Another thing to bear in mind during the sound check is clarity. Some tapes will have a bit of hiss while others may sound a little muffled. Ask your teacher if he or she can adjust any bass or treble controls (or noise reduction systems) if these are available. Students sometimes do not perform as well as they might in formal listening exercises, simply because the sound quality of what they are asked to listen to is not up to standard. So don't suffer in silence: if you cannot hear properly, then do something about it!

Step two is all about **ANTICIPATION**. This means trying to work out what you are going to hear before you even hear it; that way you are more likely to understand it completely. How can you do this? Well, it's not as difficult as it sounds. Let's take the case of a formal listening exercise, where you have to listen carefully to a text played by the teacher and then answer comprehension questions on its content. If you can, read over the questions before you start listening. Usually the questions that you will be asked will follow the order of the text; in other words, the answer to the first question will be located at the beginning of the text and the answer to the last question at the end of the text. You will find that if you read over all the questions in advance, you will get a rough idea of what the text is all about and what you have to listen for. Often a key word or expression will come up in a question, warning you in advance to listen out for it.

Let's now move on to step three, which seems quite simple—**LISTEN**. Listening, however, is an art; some people are good listeners and can easily follow the gist of what is being said, while others find it difficult to focus their attention one hundred per cent. If you are one of the latter category then try to imagine two words: *relaxed concentration*. This is the state of mind you have to be in to listen effectively. Think back to step one, and *settle yourself.* Try not to be put off your stride when the talking begins; you may be taken by surprise by the speed of delivery, but don't let it throw you. After a minute or two you will adapt to the pace; you just have to be confident that this will happen. As always, think positive—you are going to understand enough to get full marks! (This is because most formal listening exercises are devised so that you can score maximum marks without having to understand every single word.)

The second thing is *concentration*. Try to keep your mind firmly focused on the task in hand, and don't allow your mind to wander or your attention to be diverted. Constantly remind yourself of what you have to listen to. If you have a list of questions that you have to answer, then keep your eye on them all the way through the listening exercise; as I have said before, the questions often follow the order of the text and can give you hints about what to listen for. This is *anticipation* all over again—waiting for a key word or idea to come up as you sit listening to the text or conversation unfold. The more often this happens, the more confident you will get. But you have to make it happen!

One final point: listen to the different *tones of voice*. Often the sound of what someone is saying will give you an idea of what they are talking about. For example, if they raise their voice towards the end of a sentence, then it is likely that they are asking a question. They may sound surprised, annoyed, impatient, happy: all these things can give you vital clues.

Step four is all about **TRANSCRIBING** the important points of what you have heard. This can be described in simple terms as note taking. You will find that relying on your memory alone is not a good idea, especially with extended listening items. Even the best of memories can fail us on occasions, so get into the habit of jotting down notes on what you are hearing. In most cases you will not have to show these to the teacher or examiner; they are only interested in your final answers. There is no one correct way to take notes, but here are some suggestions:

• Don't include unnecessary words in your notes. Trim the note down to the bare minimum. Often one word is all you will need.

• Your notes don't have to be neat or tidy; in the words of the James Bond film, they are *for your eyes only*. There's therefore no need to worry about spellings; just take care that you can understand what you have written!

• Some students prefer to take notes in the foreign language. This can be an effective strategy as it cuts out a thought process and saves time. How? Think of it this way: if you have decided to take notes in English, you have to translate instantly in your mind the foreign word you have just heard before noting it down on paper. This can waste valuable seconds. The student who hears the foreign word and immediately writes it down (even with the wrong spelling) is at an advantage, as there will be time to translate it when they are writing up the final version of their answers. Another point: when you hear a keyword but don't know what it means, note it down phonetically—you can always ponder over what it might mean later. (In case you didn't know, writing a word phonetically means writing it as it sounds and not necessarily as it is spelled. Here's an example: the French word *généralement* could be noted down as *jane-a-ral-mon*.) It's worth doing a bit of practice on this, as it's a good skill to know in listening situations.

• Sometimes the text you are listening to will be repeated, either once or twice. In this case you can plan your note-taking strategy. You may decide to take notes during each reading of the text, or it may be better to take no notes at all during the first reading and then take notes during subsequent readings. The theory behind taking no notes the first time you hear a text is that you can concentrate fully on it, without having the distraction of trying to write down the details. Students often find that they are so busy writing down notes that they fail to listen attentively to the rest of the text, and so miss important information. Which is the best way? Unfortunately, there is no easy answer.

All I can suggest is that you try out both methods and decide which one is most effective for you.

We now come to step five, the final one. You have stopped listening to the text, and now you have the task of referring to your notes and **INTERPRETING** what you have just heard. Read over any specific questions you may have to answer and try to link them to any notes you have taken. Keep thinking back to the text you have just heard; this way you will keep it fresh in your mind. When you are ready to give your answers (either orally or in written form), report back in short, concise phrases: these are much easier to understand than long, elaborate sentences, and are much simpler for teachers to mark. If you have to hand in your written answers, then don't forget to score out any rough notes you may have taken on your answer sheet, so that these do not get confused with the fair version of your answers.

How can you best remember these five steps and the order in which they come? It's simple; just think of the word **SALTY,** only spelled like this: **SALTI.** Here's a reminder of what each letter stands for:

- **Settle** yourself.

- **Anticipate** what you are about to hear.

- **Listen** attentively.

- **Transcribe** what you hear.

- **Interpret** what you've heard.

Once you use this a few times it'll become second nature and you won't need to think about it.

Work On Your Listening Skills

It is vital that you regularly practise your listening skills outside the classroom. Your teacher will undoubtedly be doing a lot of work on listening during his or her lessons, but it's always a good idea to go one step further by doing some extra listening on your own. This way you will be able to build up your confidence in the comfort of your own home, without the usual stresses and strains that are often part of formal classroom listening situations. Here is some advice on how best you can do this:

- **Identify your listening.** If you are following a course, try to get a copy of the listening materials from your teacher. This way you can replay items you may already have done in class or practise new ones. Most courses include a lot more listening than the teacher is able to do in class, so there should be plenty to get on with. If you will be sitting a formal or public examination in the language, then get a copy of the listening past papers and do any that your teacher might have omitted in class. Most teachers will be only too happy to correct your answers as long as you hand them in regularly.

- **View the transcript.** Seeing the text before or after listening to it can be a great way of improving your listening skills. To do this you have to get access to the transcript of the listening item you are going to do. If the item comes from your coursebook, then a transcript will probably not be available, as these are normally included in the teacher's book only. If this is the case, then ask your teacher for a copy. As for books of past papers, there should be no problem here as transcripts are usually provided. Once you have your transcript, you can use it in a number of different ways:

  - Look briefly at it before the listening exercise begins but not during it.

  - Look at it in detail after you complete the listening exercise.

  - After you complete the listening exercise, listen to it again while reading the transcript (I encourage my students to do this as often as possible because reading the text as you listen to it means that the sounds of words are being linked in your head with their spellings; this in turn can improve your writing as well as your listening skills).

  - Read the transcript and note down new vocabulary and constructions you come across.

  - Use it as a translation exercise.

- **Vary your listening.** Make sure that you have enough variety in your listening. By this I mean that you should be listening to lots of different voices, speaking at different speeds in all kinds of situations. The course you are following should have a wide range of listening items, such as talks, dialogues, conversations, transactional situations, interviews, and so on. (These may also be graded at different levels of difficulty.) If you get the chance to practise extra listening, don't always stick to the same types just because you find you do quite well in them. Be adventurous; go for the longer, faster, more difficult items. If you find it's getting too much for you, then remember that *you* are in control. You can stop the tape or CD, play it again, fast-forward, rewind, or give up and try again later. Taking a relaxed and common-sense approach will improve your listening skills, but bear in mind that you do need challenge, otherwise you will always remain at the same level and never improve. One other idea: why not listen to songs in the foreign language? If you enjoy music then it's an excellent way of picking up the language, especially if you can follow the lyrics as they are being sung. (I am a big opera fan and I remember learning a lot of French and Italian by reading the *libretti* (i.e. the text the characters are singing) while I listened to the music—highly recommended!)

- **Listen with your eyes.** Remember that old saying *seeing is believing*? I tell my students than as far as listening to a foreign language is concerned, *seeing is understanding*. Let me explain: listening to someone you can see is much easier than listening to the voice only. This is because when people speak they use their bodies to give the listener visual clues about what they are saying. Their facial expressions may give away their feelings, or they may use hand movements or other body language to reinforce their message. The experts call these *paralinguistic gestures*, and they are a great help in understanding what people are trying to say. If you are in a situation where you can see the person or persons to whom you are listening (for example during a conversation or while viewing a video extract), then use your eyes to help you understand what is said. Think of it this way: most people use two languages while talking—their own language and a universal one called *sign language*. What you don't understand in one you will probably pick up in the other, so keep your eyes as well as your ears wide open.

- **Link listening with viewing.** The importance of being able to see someone while listening to them should be reflected in your practice materials. As well as listening to tapes and CD's you should also try to improve your listening skills by including the following activities (remember that further help on using technology is given in Part Four of this book):

  - **Watching video/DVD in the foreign language.** You will often have access to subtitles that you can use as you wish to check your understanding.

  - **Watching live television.** Many foreign television channels are now available through satellite and cable.

  - **Using computer language learning software.** These often have video clips that you can use to practise listening. A transcript and comprehension questions will often be provided.

  - **Listen while you talk.** Get involved in as many conversations as you can in the foreign language. Remember that talking to someone involves listening skills: after all, if you don't listen to what the other person is saying, how can you reply to them? In this respect listening and speaking are closely linked; by practising your conversational skills you are automatically becoming a better listener.

- **Learn vocabulary.** Finally, bear in mind that you cannot listen effectively if you lack a wide vocabulary base. Listening is not the type of activity where you can normally rush off and consult a dictionary if there are words you do not understand; you simply don't have time to do this! There really is no substitute for learning your vocabulary; after all, the more words and expressions you know, the better chance you will have of understanding what you hear.

The Final Word

We have talked in this chapter about two main areas: *effective listening techniques* (i.e. the five steps) and *how best to practise*. If you follow the advice I have given you will find that you will be able to listen to and understand the language you're learning much more effectively. However, let me leave you with one final thought: good listeners are those who make the effort to listen *all the time*, and not only when they are listening to the foreign language. So listen to your teacher, to your parents, to your friends—listen to everything that people say to you, and you will learn a great deal. Listening is an art that has to be learnt and practised, whatever the language. As Frank Tyger once said, *Be a good listener. Your ears will never get you in trouble.*

Speaking

Ask anyone which skill they admire most in someone who has learnt a foreign language and they will usually give the same answer: speaking. There is something about a person's ability to speak fluently in another language that never fails to impress us. It may be their confidence, their skill at speaking without apparent thought or effort, their accent, their speed of delivery. We think to ourselves: that person is an excellent *linguist*. (It is no coincidence that the root of this word is the Latin *lingua*, meaning a tongue.)

The ability to communicate with others through speech will always be regarded highly (and rightly so), but this very fact can sometimes put pressure on those of us trying to learn a foreign language. We may feel that our speaking skills are the only ones that really count, and that people will ultimately judge our linguistic ability on how well we converse in the foreign language. Obviously things are not quite as simple as this. To be a complete linguist you not only require good speaking skills, but also good listening, reading and writing skills. But the fact remains that speaking effectively in the foreign language will always be regarded as the key skill we must all possess.

Just imagine a world where no-one could speak; what kind of world would it be? For a start, we would have nothing to listen to except music and the sounds around us. We would be forced to communicate through sign language and reading and writing notes to one another. How would you find that? Your reply will depend on the kind of person you are. More than any other skill, effective speaking depends on your personality; you may be a quiet, shy individual who doesn't really like to talk to others. You would then find the world I have just described quite attractive. Or you might be confident, self-assured and assertive, in which case you will enjoy talking to everyone, and a world without conversation would be most unwelcome.

The purpose of this chapter is to help you to speak more effectively in the foreign language, whatever kind of person you are. The important thing is to remember that as with everything in life, you can improve if you put your mind to it. All you need to do is to put in the necessary time and effort!

Types of Speaking

There are two main types of speaking that you will encounter in learning a foreign language:

- **Prepared speaking**, where you know in advance what you will have to talk about, and are able to think about what you are going to say. Many of the speaking exercises you practise in class are of this type, such as role-plays, solo talks, transactional dialogues and single-topic conversations. What they all have in common is that they are highly-structured, so you know what you have to say and when to say it—it's all fairly predictable, and there are usually no unpleasant surprises. You normally receive help and advice from your teacher and are given time to prepare, after which you get a chance to practise with either the teacher or a fellow student. Depending on the speaking task, you may be allowed to refer to written notes. The last stage is delivering your final version, which may be assessed by the teacher and/or recorded.

- **Unprepared speaking**, where you either have only a rough idea of what you have to talk about or no idea at all. This type of speaking requires you to think on your feet—in other words, to react instantly to what people are saying to you. Unprepared speaking makes greater demands on your listening comprehension skills; after all, you cannot continue a conversation unless you have listened to and understood the other person. Examples you might encounter in class include open-ended conversations with either your teacher or the foreign language assistant, speaking tests that cover a variety of different subjects and role plays or transactional dialogues that suddenly go off on an unexpected tangent. Outside class, this is the type of *real* speaking you will have to deal with when you communicate with native speakers. Needless to say, there is no opportunity to rehearse or to refer to notes—this is speaking at its most natural and unpredictable, and you have to rely on the constructions and vocabulary you have inside your head, and on your ability to string them all together. You usually have only one chance to get it right, which can be quite intimidating if you are being assessed by your teacher or an examiner!

So how can you make sure that you maximise your speaking skills whatever the type of speaking situation? One approach is to use what I call the *Seven Speaking Strategies*. These are seven key areas that you should be aware of when speaking in the foreign language. They cover all aspects of good practice; in other words, they describe what effective speakers do when they communicate with others. By adopting the strategies described below we can all improve our speaking skills to a considerable extent.

Before we examine each in greater detail, I should perhaps add that the strategies are not presented in order of importance. This is because as foreign language learners we are all individuals with different strengths and weaknesses; it is up to you to decide which strategies you should concentrate on. What you should not forget is that they are all *equally* important. Like the title of a famous Hollywood western, they are without a doubt *The Magnificent Seven*.

The Seven Speaking Strategies

Let's start off with **SPEED**. Effective speaking does not necessarily mean speaking as fast as possible. Many students believe that being *fluent* in a language means being able to talk quickly. They think that the faster they go, the more impressed the listener will be. What happens? They very often cannot keep up the pace and start to make mistakes. Others students talk fast because they are nervous. They may feel uncomfortable when they speak in the foreign language and subconsciously speed up so as to get the whole thing over and done with. Whatever the situation, it pays to remember one thing: *speed kills*.

So the next time you speak in the foreign language, think to yourself: am I going too fast? If you are, then slow down! After all, you are not in a race, and whoever is listening to you is unlikely to be in a great hurry. Bear in mind that when you talk at a relaxed, moderate pace you can make yourself understood much more easily; people will be able to follow whatever it is you are saying without having to stop you and ask you to repeat something they haven't picked up. You can also slow yourself down by using what I call *delaying tactics*; this involves stopping the conversation momentarily by using phrases such as *Wait a minute.../Let me think about that.../That's interesting.../Let me tell you this...*and so on. This type of phrase can buy you precious seconds of thinking time.

The next strategy we're going to look at is **PARAPHRASE**. This is when we rephrase something we are saying in order to make it more understandable to the listener. During the course of a conversation we may fail to pick up what the other person is telling us, only to realise what it is when they use another form of words. This skill is an important one as the whole purpose of speaking is to *communicate* with others. If we do not achieve communication, then the fault may lie in the words or expressions we have chosen to use. For communication to succeed, we have to find a different way of expressing the same idea. This can be difficult when speaking in a foreign language, as we often do not have the same range of vocabulary or fluency as in our native language. The solution is to try to practise the art of paraphrase. Look at this sentence:

Can you tell me how I can get to the station?

Imagine you are trying to say this in the foreign language but cannot remember the expression *Can you tell me…* Why not try a paraphrase? An alternative way of asking the same question is to phrase it differently. Here are some examples:

How do I find the station?/I'm looking for the station.
Where is the station?/Is the station this way?
Where do I get the train?

(The last of these is the one you should use if you can't remember the word for a *station!*)

As you can see, there are often different ways of saying the same thing, and it doesn't even matter too much if your paraphrase is not strictly grammatical or what the locals would say—the main thing is that you are managing to communicate. After all, you have a train to catch and have to find the station. When all else fails, all you have to do is walk up to a stranger and say in an enquiring voice, *The station?* Or how about *The train?* The chances are that the person will realise what your problem is and give you the necessary directions. So try to get into the habit of practising your paraphrasing skills. Take a series of sentences in the foreign language and see if you can express them in other words. It'll be difficult at first, but persevere. Get your teacher to help you and you'll soon find that paraphrasing is a great tool for practising the language you already know, as well as learning new ways of expressing yourself.

My third strategy can be summed up by the word **ENTERPRISE**. This covers a number of different areas, but all of them have one thing in common: they involve you, the speaker, taking individual responsibility for your own performance. This is how you can achieve this:

- **Take the initiative.** Speaking is a dynamic activity; you only get out of it what you put in. Let me give you an example; have you ever tried to have a conversation with someone who gives one-word answers? It can be very difficult, if not impossible. To speak well in any language you have to take the lead and make the effort to communicate. Don't be afraid; the other person is not going to bite you! Say something, anything, and make sure you say it first. Break the ice and get talking; once you get over the initial fear of starting a conversation you will find that the rest flows naturally. Be adventurous and forthcoming, push yourself forward and make sure the other person has your attention. Avoid silence at all costs!

- **Forget about error.** Don't become obsessed with grammatical accuracy when you are speaking. It is far better to make the effort to communicate even if what you say has a few mistakes in it. At least you're talking, and the chances are that the other person will still be able to understand you. As I've said before, speaking is all about communication; if this doesn't take place, then there is no point to it. Remember also that you can use your mistakes positively and learn from them. Sometimes when conversing in the foreign language we realise that we have said something that is incorrect, but still manage to get our point across and so keep the conversation going. What then happens is that the person to whom we are talking will then use the proper form of words to say the same thing, allowing us to correct our mistake. I often tell my students that the errors they make in learning a foreign language are often the most valuable lessons they will receive; but if you refuse to make mistakes by keeping your mouth shut, then when are you ever going to learn anything?

- **Help yourself.** Sometimes in the course of a conversation you can get into a bit of trouble. It may be that the other person is talking too fast; if this is the case, don't be afraid to ask them to slow down. That way you'll find it easier to understand what they are saying and be more able to respond to it. There may also be a point in the conversation where you cannot understand something. What many people tend to do in such situations is to smile and pretend that they have understood, with the result that they eventually lose track of the conversation. It's much better to swallow your pride and ask for help: something along the lines of *Excuse me, I didn't understand that, could you repeat it?* That way you get a second chance to figure out what the other person is trying to tell you. The final tip I'm going to give you regards asking questions. Sometimes in a conversation you may find that you are running out of things to say. The other person may be showing no sign of wanting to take over and is happy to let you talk. What do you do? The answer is to hit the ball back into the other person's court by asking a question. This does two things: it relieves the immediate pressure on yourself and also gives you a chance to think about what you are going to say next.

Let's now talk about **CLARITY**. What I mean by this is how effectively and clearly you use your voice. Start off by reminding yourself what the purpose of speaking is. As I have said earlier in this chapter, it is to *communicate*. Two things have to happen if communication is to take place when we speak: we have to find the correct form of words, and then we have to *deliver* them. It is no use knowing what you have to say if you cannot say it clearly and distinctly enough to be understood. Many students concentrate exclusively on the content of what they are going to say, without giving any thought as to how they are going to put it across. The result is speaking that is often indistinct and lacking in conviction. What happens? The listener can find it difficult to follow and at the worst, will lose interest. This can be avoided by making sure that your voice delivery is up to scratch. Here are the points to watch:

- **Are you loud enough?** The volume of your voice is important, especially if you are talking to a large audience. Those of us who don't have loud voices needn't worry; you will still be heard if you can *project* your voice adequately. This is a technique that can be learnt or acquired through experience; your teacher may be able to help you with it.

- **Are you distinct enough?** For other people to understand you properly you have to pay attention to your *enunciation*. This is the measure of how clearly you say your words. Another way of describing it is *good diction*. Simply stated, it involves making sure that each word you say is distinctly sounded so that it can be made out from the other words in the sentence. After all, if the words you say are indistinct and run into each other, people will find them difficult to comprehend. Think of the problems you have trying to follow someone who mumbles and mutters; this is because you cannot understand enough individual words to make sense of the overall message.

- **How's your pronunciation?** This is all about knowing exactly how individual words are *said*. Depending on the language you are learning, the spelling may often indicate how the word is to be pronounced. Indeed, the longer you learn a language the easier it becomes to look at new words and pronounce them successfully. If you are just beginning to learn a language, then you will have to rely mostly on listening attentively to your teacher and repeating the correct pronunciation. Remember that when you're talking, it generally doesn't make a great deal of difference if you mispronounce the occasional word—the listener will usually get the overall message.

- **What about your accent?** A great accent is obviously a plus when you are talking in the foreign language. Listen as much as you can to native speakers and try to imitate them. The more you do this, the quicker you will begin to sound authentic. Some students (especially male) feel self-conscious when they attempt to imitate an accent; they think that their fellow students will find it pretentious and make fun of them. All I can say here is forget about other people and have a go. (After all, if you were constantly to worry about what other people say, then you would never do anything worthwhile in life!) One final thing: you don't have to talk with a perfect accent in order to be understood. So don't get too hung up about it—at the end of the day, it's what you say that counts, and how clearly you get the message across. Concentrate on this, and with time the accent will take care of itself.

- **How's your tone of voice?** The tone that you use when you talk in the foreign language is crucially important. Ask yourself what makes a person's voice sound *monotonous*: it's when they talk constantly in the one tone, without ever trying to change it. (In case you hadn't noticed, the word *monotonous* is made up of two others: *mono,* meaning one, and *tone.*) Obviously anyone talking like this will soon alienate the listener (or even worse, send them to sleep). The trick is to *vary* the tone of your voice as you speak. Think of music, with its high notes, its low notes, its short phrases, its longer phrases. It's a language all in itself! So when you want to make an important point, bring that across in your voice by sounding forceful and authoritative. If you want to convince someone to do something, sound persuasive. When you ask a question, raise the tone of your voice as you come towards the end of it. Tone is universal; even if you don't understand a single word of what someone is saying, you can still gain a rough idea by listening to the tone of their voice. So when you talk in the foreign language, do it expressively; vary your tone according to your message, and it will be delivered to your listener with the greatest of ease.

Our next strategy is called **INVENTIVENESS**. Effective speaking is all about avoiding the short, simplistic answer in favour of something longer and more intricate. As such, it makes demands on your ingenuity and imagination. Here are some useful pointers:

- **Go beyond the minimum.** Many speaking situations involve you having to talk at some length. For example, you may be asked to deliver a short talk or presentation on a particular subject. Or in the course of a casual conversation someone might ask you about your recent holiday. How do you keep talking? One approach is to go for *detailed* answers. Let's take the holiday scenario as our example. Which aspects of the holiday do you talk about? A useful device for making sure that you cover as much ground as possible is to consider these five key questions:

  - **Who?** e.g. Who went on holiday with you?
  - **What?** e.g. What did you do while you were on holiday?
  - **Where?** e.g. Where exactly did you go?
  - **When?** e.g. When did you go?
  - **Why?** e.g. Why did you go to this particular place?

If you keep these five key questions in mind while you are talking then you will have plenty of material with which to keep going. It doesn't matter which order you take them in and you don't need to cover them all; it all depends on the speaking situation and context. For example, if you are carrying on a conversation, then there may be points at which it would be inappropriate to give this degree of detail; you just have to use your common sense. But in those cases where you are put on the spot and expected to talk away the strategy I've described can be invaluable. (I'll show you later on how you can best practise this technique. It also comes in very useful when you are writing creatively in the foreign language, as we shall see in another chapter.)

One further point: just because you are trying to say more does not mean that you should be over-ambitious. In situations where you are being assessed it pays to stick to what you know, rather than try to say things of which you are unsure. I always tell my students to *keep it simple*; in other words, use the language with which they are most familiar and comfortable. There will be plenty other occasions in the future when they can afford to be a little more adventurous.

- **Be economical with the truth.** This piece of advice might sound a bit doubtful, but I can assure you that in the right circumstances it is an effective technique. Imagine you are in the middle of a speaking test, and the teacher asks you what your parents do for a living. It may be that your father is a quantity surveyor and your mother a mortgage advisor, but you don't know how to express this in the foreign language. Rather than panic, be economical with the truth by making your father a doctor and your mother a teacher. This way you keep talking; eventually the conversation will move on and you will have side-stepped a potentially tricky moment. We all live complicated lives, and sometimes trying to describe aspects of them accurately in the foreign language can be beyond our powers. In a situation such as a speaking test the absolute truth of what you say is not important; what the examiner is assessing is your overall ability in speaking the language. Don't worry if you feel uncomfortable with the whole idea of substituting fact for fiction; there are a couple of other possibilities. In the above scenario you could always ask, in the foreign language, how you say *quantity surveyor* and *mortgage advisor* and rely on the other person to tell you; alternatively, you could try describing in the foreign language what each job involves.

Here's the next of our seven strategies: **ATTENTIVENESS.** By this I mean using our listening skills in order to improve the quality of our speaking. As you know, having an effective conversation depends on our ability to listen to what the other person is saying and to react to it accordingly. In my experience many students fail to do this when they are conversing in the foreign language; they are so focused on what they want to say that they do not really listen to what the other person says in return. The result is a one-sided, meaningless conversation where there is no interaction between the speakers. In the worst cases the conversation can degenerate into a monologue that the listener gives up trying to interrupt.

The lesson to be learnt here is to pay attention to the other half of the conversation and to respond to it. Taking the time to stop and listen can help you in turn to talk freely and naturally. It's called the art of conversation! There is one other thing that I'd like to mention here. I've already said that you should listen to other people while you are talking to them. If that person is your teacher or a native speaker then you should go one stage further: after the conversation has taken place (and it is still fresh in your mind) note down any new vocabulary or turns of phrase that you learned from it. This way you can try them out yourself the next time you talk.

We now come to the final strategy: **LIVELINESS**. Speaking is, by its very nature, the most extrovert of the four key skills; it involves you interacting with other people, something you don't always have to do when listening, reading or writing. Those of us who are warm, friendly, outgoing and full of confidence are probably at a bit of an advantage here. But whatever your personality, you have to ensure that when you talk you have that added spark of vitality and liveliness that makes others want to listen and speak to you. Here are some things to watch out for:

- **Vary the tone of your voice.** I make no apologies for repeating this one, but a monotonous delivery will do you no favours.

- **Keep smiling.** Don't appear worried or nervous when you talk. Try to remain calm, be pleasant, and keep smiling.

- **Maintain your eye contact.** Look at people when you talk to them!

- **Use your body language.** Don't talk with both hands tied between your back. Use your hands to gesture and make signs, and use your face to express what you are thinking or to reinforce what you are saying. Remember that talk can be visual as well as verbal.

That completes our list of the *Seven Speaking Strategies.* How can you remember them? It's simple; think of the word **SPECIAL**:

<u>S</u>peed, <u>P</u>araphrase, <u>E</u>nterprise, <u>C</u>larity, <u>I</u>nventiveness, <u>A</u>ttentiveness, <u>L</u>iveliness.

Work On Your Speaking Skills

It's no use having a set of speaking strategies if you are not prepared to practise them. During the course of your work in class your teacher should give you plenty of opportunities to do this, but your involvement doesn't stop there—it should continue at home, even if you are on your own with no-one else to talk to. Here are some ways in which you can actively practise your speaking, both at your place of learning and at home:

- **Speak out in class.** Make the most of the speaking tasks you are given in class, especially when you are working with one other person or in a group and are unsupervised by the teacher. It is easy in such situations to slacken off and under-perform, or even worse have a casual conversation in English. Keep your mind firmly on the task in hand, and give it your all. Remember that you are at your place of learning and not in the foreign country, so the possibilities of practising your speaking are limited. Maximise those that you have!

- **Talk to the right people.** The person or group you work with can determine how effectively you practise. How comfortable do you feel with them? Obviously it's a bad idea to practise with someone with whom you don't get on. Are they the same level of ability? Working with people who are less able than you means that you cannot practise to your full potential. Similarly, if you work with fellow students who are much more capable than you are, then you may find yourself floundering. Groups can also be problematic, as sometimes there will be one dominant member who will monopolise the conversation and discourage others from participating. The best course of action is to ask your teacher for advice; that way you will be assured of working with an appropriate individual or group.

- **Expand your speaking opportunities.** Try to get some extra speaking practice at other points in the working day. Intervals, lunch-breaks, and after lessons are times when you can organise extra practice sessions. These can be with your friends or your teacher, if he or she is willing. Many places of learning also have a foreign language assistant who may agree to help out.

- **Practise at home.** There are a number of different ways of continuing your speaking practice at home. You may have a parent, brother or sister with whom you can practise; if so, get them to help you! If you are on your own, then try speaking to yourself. Draw up a list of topics that you think you can speak about. If you want, make some brief notes. Then try talking for as long as possible about it, using the five key questions I mentioned (*who, what, where, when, why*). If you can, record yourself and play it back—you can do this using either a normal tape-recorder or a compute. Another option is to keep a daily audio-diary. At the end of each day think about three things: what you are doing at that precise moment, what you have done during the day and what you will be doing tomorrow (you can make a few short notes if you wish). If you record this on a daily basis you will be able to practise speaking in the present, past and future tenses, and if you keep the recordings you can refer back to them for revision purposes. (Don't worry if you don't know all three tenses; you can do something similar with only one or two.)

- **Revise vocabulary and grammar.** As I have already said, your ability to speak relies totally on the knowledge of the language that you carry in your head—no time to look up dictionaries, check grammar points or consult with your teacher! So get into the habit of revising your vocabulary and grammar on a regular basis; after all, these are the building bricks of language, and without them all you will be able to say will be fixed, pre-learned phrases rather than sentences that you are able to formulate and construct according to your needs.

The Final Word

All I want to say here is one thing: speak as often as you can. Many years ago I spent a month in Poland with some university friends. Before I went I bought a phrase book and tried to learn some Polish, but all I could remember before my departure were three things: *tak, nie,* and *dzien dobry* (*yes, no* and *good morning*). Despite this minimal knowledge I managed to do all my holiday shopping, buy drinks in cafés, and have meals in restaurants. How did I do it? By smiling, pointing, and using the above three phrases. It was hard going and I do not recommend it, but the moral of my story is this: if I could do so much with such a limited amount of a language I had never studied, what could you achieve with your much deeper knowledge of a language that you *are* studying? The answer is a great deal, and much more than you think—so get out there and start talking!

Reading

Reading in the foreign language always gets mixed reviews from students. Some enjoy it and find it easy; when you ask them why, they will explain that the written word is there, printed in front of them, ready for them to read, re-read and ponder over. Text, unlike speech, doesn't disappear; we can come back to it as often as we want, we can read it slowly, quickly, deeply or superficially. It's always there, on the printed page or computer screen.

Other students, however, dislike reading for this very reason. It scares them to see a big chunk of text; they think to themselves, *I'll never be able to read this* and they panic. They cannot cope with masses of words all grouped together in big paragraphs, because they lack the confidence to be able to break them down and analyse their meaning. Sometimes it's a question of patience rather than confidence. Many students are naturally impatient and dislike spending time trying to decipher a text. They lose interest in any piece of writing that they cannot instantly understand.

What kind of student are you? Think about how you feel about reading in general, and not just in the foreign language. You may be a confident, adventurous reader, or an unwilling and faltering one; many of us are somewhere in the middle. The purpose of the present chapter is to give you some useful guidance about how to read effectively in the foreign language, whatever your level of ability. Where do we start? By looking at the different types of texts you will encounter.

Types of Reading

The nature of the foreign language texts that you will be expected to tackle will depend on the stage that you have reached in your studies. When choosing texts for you to read, your teacher will have taken into account such factors as length, appearance, range of vocabulary, tenses and grammatical constructions. These things all influence how easy or difficult a text is to comprehend. Sometimes texts include glossaries, pictures, and notes, all of which might help you. The conditions under which you read a text are also important: how long you have, how much help your teacher gives you, whether or not you can use a dictionary. Then there is the task you have been set: are you reading the text purely for pleasure, or must you prove that you have understood the main points by answering a series of questions? Another aspect is the medium you use to read a text. Is it printed on paper or viewed on a screen?

As you can see, reading in the foreign language can take a number of different forms, and the types of text you will encounter also vary considerably. Here are some examples:

- **Newspaper and magazine items**, such as headlines, advertisements, news items, articles, reports, surveys, horoscopes, announcements, small ads, television and radio listings, photo captions, weather forecasts, recipes, problem pages, cartoon strips.

- **Communication devices**, such as letters, postcards, invitations, greeting cards, messages, e-mails, text messages, bulletins, instructions.

- **Information and publicity items**, such as notices, leaflets, flyers, posters, displays, menus, report cards, financial statements, bills, receipts.

- **Literary items**, such as books, novels, poems, short stories, essays, readers; either full-length or extracts.

The thing that becomes apparent from this list is the sheer variety of text types and lengths. As I have already stated, it is the extended texts (i.e. those longer than a single paragraph) that normally cause the most problems. Most teachers ensure that their students are able to deal with these by practising formal reading comprehension exercises; in other words, texts in the foreign language followed by a series of questions to test understanding. The best way to approach these is to use a technique that I call the *Five Phases of Effective Reading.* If you follow these through (one after the other, in the precise order in which they are listed) then you will find it easier to tackle reading comprehension exercises, as well as learning more about the language contained within them. (You can also use the same technique for casual reading; just ignore any references to answering questions.)

The Five Phases of Effective Reading

The first phase asks you to **RELATE** to the text. By this I mean gathering together your first impressions. Start by *looking* at the text. Don't read it at this stage; just *look* at it. Then ask yourself these questions:

- **What type of text is it?** A first glance should tell you what type of text you have to deal with. Sometimes the text will be preceded by a short introductory note in English that can give you valuable information on what you are about to read.

- **Does it have a title and/or subtitle?** Look at the main title first. Does it contain any clues about the content of the passage? Now check if there are any subtitles; these are normally placed below the main title and may be in a smaller and/or different font. Subtitles are useful because they often summarise the key points of a text, thus giving the reader an advance preview of the content.

- **How long is the text?** Quickly check the length of the text. This will give you a rough idea of how long it will take you to read it and answer any questions. If you are doing an examination paper with a series of reading items, look at them all so that you can calculate the approximate length of time to spend on each.

- **What are the questions like?** Most of the reading exercises you will be given take the form of a text followed by a series of comprehension questions, either in English or in the foreign language. These questions may require either a spoken or written response from you. Occasionally, the questions may be followed by a variety of possible answers of which one only is correct (this format is called *multiple choice*). Usually you will be told the number of points a question is worth. At this point just glance quickly at the questions; you will be looking at them more closely during the next stage.

- **Are there any pictures that accompany the text?** A picture is worth a thousand words. Take a good look at them; they may contain useful clues or hints. But remember that they can sometimes be misleading; after all, it is the *text* that you are expected to understand. You can't pass just by looking at a picture!

- **Do these pictures have captions?** If so, then great; read the captions and relate them to the picture. I have come across many reading exercises where the answer to a question was to be found in a caption rather than in the main body of the text. You ignore them at your peril!

- **Is there a glossary to help you with unfamiliar words?** In case you didn't know, a glossary is a list of words and expressions that occur in the text, and for which you are given either an English translation or an explanation in the foreign language. Most glossaries are placed at the end of the text, but despite this they can be easily overlooked. Many of my students have completed their answers to a reading comprehension exercise only to realise that there was a glossary giving them the meanings of key words; the same words that they had spent a lot of time looking up in the dictionary! Glossaries are a valuable asset; make sure that you take advantage of them.

Now let's move onto the second phase. This requires you to form an **OUT-LINE** of the text in your head; not a detailed knowledge of its content, but what we might call an *overall picture*. This is how it should be done (try to follow these steps in the order in which they are listed):

- **Read the questions a first time.** Read any comprehension questions carefully before you read the text. These can give you a good idea of what the text is all about and what you should look out for. The questions will normally follow the order of the text, so you can reasonably assume that the answer to question one will be found at the beginning of the text, and the answer to the last question towards the end. Sometimes you will be referred to a particular paragraph or point in the text; this makes things even easier.

- **Skim read the text.** This is an important technique that involves reading the text quickly so as to form a rough idea of its content. Don't stop and ponder over individual words and phrases of which you're unsure, or be tempted to use a dictionary; what is vital at this stage is that you get an overall impression. However, if you spot a word or expression that is new to you and the meaning suddenly comes into your head, then note it down quickly before you forget it. (This is especially important if you are working under test conditions without a dictionary.)

- **Identify key sections.** Now refer back to the questions and then *scan* the text. This means reading through the text quickly in order to locate those parts where you think the answers might lie. Once again, don't ponder over individual words or phrases and don't use the dictionary. Sometimes you will spot a word or phrase that contains an answer; other times it may be an entire paragraph. You should then mark these parts of the text either by underlining them or by using a highlighter; this ensures that you will be able to find them again without having to search through large chunks of text. (A word of advice: check with your teacher that you are able to do this. Marking the text with pens or highlighters may not be permitted, as another student may have to use the same copy. In this case you may be able to mark the text lightly with a pencil and rub it out afterwards.)

Phase three now asks you to read in **DETAIL**. Here's how to do this (once again, follow the steps in the proper order):

- **Re-read the entire text.** Start at the beginning and read the text continuously, slowly and carefully all the way through to the end.

- **Examine the key sections.** Now look back at the sections you marked when you scanned the text. Read each of these in turn, referring back to the relevant question(s) to remind yourself of what they are asking you to do. If you have a dictionary, use it only to look up those words and expressions that you feel are necessary for your complete understanding (effective dictionary technique is described in the chapter *Using a Dictionary*). If you don't have a dictionary, then you will have to rely on what I call the *Triple S Test* to work out the meanings of words you don't know.

  The first *S* stands for *Similarity*: does the word look like any other word you know in English or any other language you are studying? If it does, it is likely to have the same meaning. (But beware of *false friends*; these are words that look as if they have the same meaning but actually mean something totally different.) If it is a long word, is it made up of a series of smaller words you might recognise? Does it have a prefix or suffix that might give a clue to its meaning? (If you don't know what I mean by this, then ask your teacher.)

  The second *S* stands for *Sound*: sometimes the sound of a word can give a clue to its meaning. This can work in two different ways: either the sound will be linked directly to the meaning (this is called *onomatopoeia*; think of English words such as *buzz* or *hiss*) or the sound will remind you of a word you already know in English or another foreign language that you are studying.

  The third *S* stands for *Surrounding*: what this means is that you shouldn't always look at problem words in isolation. Consider the language that *surrounds* them; it's here that you may find clues to their meaning. Think of it this way; if someone gave you a single flower petal instead of the whole flower, would you know which flower it had come from? It's the same with language; single words can mean very little to us if they are separated from their *context*.

So when you are trying to figure out that single, mystery word, look at the language that comes before it and after it; that's where you'll probably find the solution.

- **Finalise your answers.** The last stage is to answer the comprehension questions. Try to bear the following things in mind as you do this:

  - Be relevant! Make sure that you answer the question. The number of points it is worth should give you some idea of the level of detail required. Don't include any extra details that may have nothing to do with the original question.

  - Present your answers clearly and logically. Stick to the point and never give alternative answers.

  - If you are writing your answers, you might consider writing notes rather than sentences, but take care that you avoid ambiguity and include the right amount of detail. Avoid translating chunks of the text and presenting them as answers; this doesn't always prove that you have understood the question.

  - We now come to the end of the third phase: so far you have read the text, understood its overall meaning, looked in detail at its most important features and answered comprehension questions. The remaining two phases revisit the text to make sure that you *learn* from what you have read.

Phase four invites you to **EXPLORE** the text. By this I mean looking over the language used by the author and asking yourself the following questions:

- **Which new words and expressions have I come across?** We may discover new vocabulary and idioms any time we read in the foreign language. If you have not already done so, underline or highlight these in the text.

- **Are there any new grammar points?** You may have spotted unfamiliar constructions that you don't fully understand. Once again, underline or highlight these.

- **Is there a part of the text I think I could translate?** Many courses neglect the teaching of translation skills. Why not get some practice yourself? Pick a paragraph or a series of sentences and get busy translating. Show your work to your teacher once you've finished.

We now arrive at the fifth and final phase. What I am now suggesting is that you should now **ORGANISE** what you have learnt from your reading of the text so that you have a permanent and accessible record of it. This way you will be able to refer back and revise all the more easily.

Let's start with the new vocabulary and idioms you have come across. These should be noted down in the vocabulary section of your languages file (see pages 33–34). The best way to do this is to divide each of your vocabulary pages into two columns; put the foreign language item on the left and the English translation on the right. Some students like to add a third column for extra information; this might include notes about how to use the word or expression, how to pronounce it, which text it occurred in, and so on. Do this methodically and on a regular basis, and within a short time you will have a valuable bank of useful vocabulary and expressions. One last thing: it's good to note it all down, but not so good if you never look at it again. So get into the habit of regularly reading over your collection; dip into it from time to time for words and phrases to use in your speaking and writing assignments; add to it at every available opportunity.

The next thing you should do is to note in your grammar file any new constructions you identified in the text. At this stage you may be unsure of how a particular grammar point works and how you should note it down; if this is the case, then ask your teacher. He or she will either explain it to you in person or refer you to the relevant section of your textbook. Once you understand it you can write it down in your own words together with a few examples of how it is used.

Finally, you will remember my suggestion that you translate parts of the reading texts that you do. It is important that you get your teacher to correct your translation, so that you can do a second and better version if necessary. When you are satisfied with your translation file it alongside a copy of the original foreign language text; that way you can read over both of them at a later date and remind yourself of the vocabulary and expressions used by the original author.

Let's now remind ourselves of the *Five Phases of Effective Reading* I have just described. Here they are again:

- **RELATE** to the text.

- Look at the **OUTLINE**.

- Consider the **DETAIL**.

- **EXPLORE** new language.

- **ORGANISE** what you've learnt.

In case you hadn't noticed, the first letter of each key word spells out **RODEO.** Where's the connection? Well, the next time you do a reading comprehension, I want you to imagine you're riding a wild horse. In the best cowboy tradition, don't let it throw you: *rodeo* it into submission!

Work On Your Reading Skills

During the course of your work in class your teacher will practise reading skills with you, and may also give you reading comprehension exercises as homework. But it shouldn't stop there; if you are serious about developing your reading skills then you must get in some extra practice of your own. Here are some ways in which you can do this:

- **Consult your teacher**. It makes sense to involve your teacher, as he or she has a close knowledge of your ability and can suggest extra pieces of reading for you to do at home. Most teachers are only too willing to do this and will offer to correct any extra work. The great advantage of this approach is that you don't have to spend time searching on your own for extra pieces of reading.

- **Find your own texts.** As we saw at the beginning of the chapter, reading texts come in many different shapes and forms. There are two basic questions that you have to ask yourself if you are selecting your own extra reading:

  - *What type of reading am I looking for?*
  - *Where can I find it?*

    Let's deal with the first question. Start by examining your motives for wanting to read more in the foreign language; it may be that you require more practice at reading comprehension, or you just want to read for pleasure and learn something along the way. If you choose the reading comprehension route, then your teacher is the obvious source of suitable materials. If you decide to read for pleasure, then there is a lot of material that you can easily access on your own.

    This brings us nicely onto the second question. The obvious problem most students have in finding extra reading materials is that they are not living in the country whose language they are studying; consequently, they have to make do with what they can find locally. Here, then, are some places where you may be able to access additional reading materials:

- **Your place of learning or local library.** Many libraries now have large collections of foreign language texts, ranging from newspapers and magazines to full-length novels. Sometimes you will have to consult these in the library but you may also be able to borrow them. Ask your librarian for more information.

- **Bookshops.** Larger bookshops often have a foreign languages section. If you decide you want to spend money on a book then it's best to ask your teacher's advice; it may be that there are suitable books on the market that your teacher cannot supply you with in your place of learning. After all, you don't want to waste money buying something that you'll not be able to read!

- **Newsagents.** The bigger newsagents often carry a selection of foreign language newspapers and magazines. Newspapers are quite a good buy as they are often not as expensive as magazines and are much more topical, as well as having a wider range of articles of different lengths. One strategy I recommend to students is to buy a foreign language newspaper but to avoid reading it until they have watched on television the international news in English for that day. They then look at any equivalent news items in the newspaper they have just bought; in this way they are able to understand a lot more, as they are already aware of the main features and details of the various news stories. You can use magazines in a similar way. Let's say that you are really interested in cars. Why not try to get a car magazine in the foreign language? You'll find that you can understand most of the car descriptions and reviews simply because you've read about the same cars in English and are already familiar with their features. One other thing; both newspapers and magazines have plenty of advertisements—read them all! Advertisements in the foreign language are great reading, because they are visual and we may already have seen English versions for the same products. Finally, don't forget the old favourites: weather forecasts, horoscopes, recipes, television guides, problem pages, and recipes. All human life is there, and you'll also learn a lot about the language!

- **The Internet.** The Internet is an excellent source of reading materials of all descriptions, but its sheer size often makes finding suitable items quite daunting. What I suggest you do is read over pages 130–131 where I explain how to get the best results from your time on-line.

- **Everyday objects.** The foreign language is all around us, and often we don't realise it! Here is an example: if you buy something that comes with instructions, take the time to read them—and not just in English. Many instruction leaflets and guarantees are printed in a number of foreign languages. This can give us valuable reading practice and the opportunity to compare the English version to its foreign language equivalent. It doesn't stop there; when you're having breakfast, read the side of the cereal packet, as the list of ingredients is often given in different foreign languages. Even the labels on your clothes can hide valuable little pieces of the foreign language. So look everywhere, and you will find reading practice in the most unusual and unexpected of places.

- **Read imaginatively.** Many students do not realise that there are many different forms of reading. Here are some suggestions; why not try some of them out?

  - **Read aloud.** Reading aloud in the foreign language is a skill often neglected by students. This is unfortunate, since there are three distinct advantages to this approach. The first is that when you read something aloud, you hear the sound of the words and this can often help you to understand the meaning. The second is that you gain valuable pronunciation practice, while the third is increased self-confidence. Another thing that you can do is to record yourself. One technique I recommend is what I call the *Four R's*: read aloud, record, replay and recall. This is what it involves: first of all decide what portion of the text you are going work with and read it over silently. Then try reading it aloud, but don't record yourself until you feel confident enough. Once you finish your recording replay it and, if necessary, re-record it. Then leave it for a day or two and then come back to it; this time replay the recording *without* looking at the text, and see how much of its meaning you can recall. After you do this play the recording one last time but this time read the text as you listen. The entire process is an effective one because it combines reading, speaking and listening practice, as well as making it easier for you to remember any new language presented in the text.

  - **Read and view.** It's a well-known fact that young children prefer texts that have pictures in them. We can all remember flicking through books, looking at the pictures and ignoring the words. Sometimes this was enough to follow the story, but other times we had to get an adult to read it to us. What I am going to suggest is that you practise reading in the foreign language by finding texts that are heavily illustrated. Examples of such texts are comics, cartoon strips, photo stories (such as those in teenage magazines) and children's storybooks. These are ideal since the text and illustrations go hand in hand; what you don't understand in the text will probably be apparent in the illustration, and vice versa. This combination of text and image is a powerful aid to understanding. If you have read the chapter on listening, you will remember that watching people's body language can often help us to comprehend what they are saying. Here we have much the same process; we read the words while looking at the picture, and our brain makes the right connections. So try to *read and view* as much as you can, and you'll develop what I call *double vision*: the power to see two forms of the same message and arrive at a single conclusion about them. One final point: the great thing about read and view is the texts. Comics, cartoon strips and children's stories are all entertaining and lightweight reading, especially if you already know the characters and situations from reading the English versions. To rephrase a famous proverb, *Familiarity breeds comprehension.*

- **Read with ease.** Longer texts, such as short stories and novels, can often seem intimidating to the foreign language learner. What many students require when tackling texts of this kind is continuous support, either from their teacher or the dictionary (and often both). Bear in mind, however, that there may be simplified and shortened versions of the same novels and stories available (one well-known series goes by the name of *Easy Readers*). These are often graded by level of difficulty so that you can pick one that you'll be able to cope with. If you have to read a literary text in the original version then you may find that there are special student editions available: these will often have useful features such as an introduction, explanatory footnotes and a glossary. Some publishers also issue what are known as *parallel texts*: these consist of the foreign language on the left-hand page and an English translation on the right-hand page. So if you don't understand something while reading in the foreign language, all you do is look across! Finally, I would like to encourage you to try reading through a really long text in the foreign language; be brave and decide that you're going to have a go. Ask your teacher to recommend something to you, possibly an easy reader or a parallel text; you'll enjoy it, and the sense of achievement you'll feel when you complete it will make the effort worthwhile.

The Final Word

I tell my students that to improve their reading skills in the foreign language they have to do three things:

- **Read as much as you can.** Read frequently in the foreign language, and vary the kind of texts you read. Don't forget to read as widely as you can in English, as this will help you with the foreign language.

- **Set yourself challenges.** It's no use reading texts that are too easy for you. Broaden your horizons and aim high. Try to read texts that challenge you. This is the only way that you will learn and progress.

- **Enjoy your reading.** Remember that if you enjoy reading in the foreign language, then you will learn more effectively. So bring a positive attitude to your reading. Find texts that you enjoy, and read them for pleasure.

Let me finish by quoting the famous British statesman Edmund Burke: *To read without reflecting is like eating without digesting.* You will get the most out of your reading by thinking about what you have read; so chew well, swallow carefully and you'll avoid verbal indigestion!

Writing

Writing in the foreign language is something most students enjoy. Why should this be so? Perhaps it is because the written word has authority and prestige; if something is written down it automatically assumes a degree of importance, so if you are a capable and effective writer others will admire you. Or maybe it's because writing, like speaking, is an active skill; what we are doing when we write is communicating, but in a permanent and fixed form. We therefore feel a sense of satisfaction when others read what we have written and receive our complete and detailed message.

Another possibility is that we have time to think and reflect when we write; we can take things at our own pace, choose our own ways of expressing ourselves, read over what we have written, change it if necessary and then, when we are happy with the final product, we can deliver it to our reader. Writing is the controlled recording of our thoughts, set out on paper for others to read and consider. It is this sense of being in control that appeals to many students, and makes writing in the foreign language a positive and enriching experience.

So what kind of writer are you? You may be one of those students who have plenty of ideas when writing creatively in the foreign language; you write quickly but carelessly, and your work contains frequent errors. Alternatively you may lack imagination and limit your writing to what you know to be correct; you never take risks and your work is dull, but with almost no mistakes. Or you might be in that category of students for whom writing is a pain rather than a pleasure; you have little to say, and find difficulty in saying it. Finally, you may be one of those fortunate students who are both highly imaginative and accurate in everything they write. (If this is the case, then don't stop reading; none of us is perfect and we all still have something to learn!)

Whatever type of student you are, you will find that the advice given in this chapter will help you to write more creatively while maintaining a high standard of linguistic accuracy. Where do we start? By looking at some of the different types of writing you may be expected to produce.

Types of Writing

Here are the main types of writing in the foreign language that you may encounter during the course of your studies:

- **Copy writing.** This is where your teacher asks you to copy down, word for word, a text in the foreign language. You may have to copy something from the board or from a textbook, and the texts you have to copy may be either printed, typed or hand-written. This kind of activity may seem simple, but you should take care to ensure that you copy accurately. Check spellings, accented letters and punctuation as you go along, and keep referring back to the original. This is especially important if you are copying down things like new vocabulary and phrases; remember that if you copy them down incorrectly the first time, you run the risk of repeating the error in future, especially if you refer constantly to your notes. There is also the danger that you remember the incorrect spelling rather than the correct one; as we all know, it is much harder to *unlearn* something than to learn it properly the first time around. Take care when you copy words and expressions hand-written by native speakers; handwriting styles can vary tremendously from country to country, and sometimes writers may form their letters in unfamiliar ways. It is all too easy to get caught out here, so I recommend that you acquaint yourself with the different styles of handwriting of the country whose language you are studying. Ask your teacher about this, and he or she will probably give you some extra guidance and/or practice.

- **Directed writing.** Directed writing is when you are told in detail exactly what you have to write. For example you may be asked to write a letter to reserve a room at a hotel after being given all the relevant information: type of room, length of stay, facilities in room, time of arrival, price per night, and so on. Your final letter will therefore have to include all this detail, as omitting or changing any of it could mean that the wrong reservation is made. Another possible example is a report on a recent exchange trip, where you are asked to provide the following information: how long the exchange lasted, who participated, how you travelled to the foreign country, a description of the foreign institution, which lessons you attended, what you did in your spare time, and so on. When writing your report you will have to take care to comment on all the above areas, otherwise your report will be incomplete.

In both the examples I have given the teacher has *directed* you to produce a piece of writing that is tailored to a precise specification. This limits your freedom to write freely, but the big advantage is that it provides you with a ready-made plan from which to work—this can be a real bonus if you are not particularly imaginative. The other side of the coin is that you are tied down to what you have been told to write about, and in directed writing there is often little room for manoeuvre. What happens if you have been asked to reserve a twin-bedded room with shower or bath on the second floor and you don't know the word for *shower*? The short answer is that you have to find out, otherwise the correct reservation will not be made! The lesson to be learnt from all of this is that in directed writing it is vital that you read the *specification* carefully (this is the list of things you have been told to write about). Make sure that you cover all of it in your response; if you omit parts of it or change the details then you may be penalised.

• **Creative writing.** This type of writing puts you in control, as you are asked to use your imagination to create an original piece of written work. It is perhaps the most common type of writing that you will encounter in the foreign language class; examples include letters, essays and stories. What happens here is that your teacher will give you a theme or subject to write about, together with some generalised advice or suggestions as to what you might include. Sometimes you will be given a short plan and a list of vocabulary and constructions to help you, along with an indication of how long your completed piece of writing should be. Then you are left to get on with it, and that's when the problems start for many students. We all know that familiar feeling that creeps over us when we are faced with a blank sheet of paper: *What on earth can I write?* The longer we stare at the sheet, the more anxious we become, and we soon develop what is known as *writer's block*: a total inability to find ideas and the language with which to express them. Don't let it happen to you! To help you write creatively (and accurately) I have devised a technique that I call the *Four Phases of Effective Writing*; this will enable you to adopt a structured and systematic approach to this type of written assignment.

The Four Phases of Effective Writing

The first phase asks you to **DRAFT** your piece of work. This means coming up with a first version that you can then work on in greater detail. Imagine that you are an artist painting a picture; you start with a sketch, modify it if necessary, transfer it to the canvas and apply the paint to form the final image. Writing a piece in the foreign language is very similar; you cannot put pen to paper and rustle up a masterpiece instantaneously, without any forethought. Only the most gifted linguists and writers can do this, and even then it requires great mental effort along with a good dose of inspiration. The rest of us should take things one step at a time, starting with a first draft. There are several stages that you have to go through in order to produce this, and these can be listed as follows:

- **Consider the task you have been given.** Before you start writing, it pays to sit back for a moment and read over the details of what you have to write about. Look carefully at the wording of the task and make sure that you know how long your response should be. Remember that what you write has to be *relevant* to the task you have been set; marks are often deducted if you stray too far away from the subject. So keep to the point and you won't go wrong.

- **Jot down your initial ideas.** This is what I like to call *brainstorming*. Take a sheet of paper and think long and hard about what you might write. Ideas may come into your head; when they do, scribble them down quickly on the top half of the sheet. It doesn't matter too much at this stage whether your notes are in English or in the foreign language; just get them down on paper, and don't worry about whether or not they are in the right order. What happens if you don't have any ideas? No problem: think back to the advice I gave in the chapter on speaking (pages 51–52). You will remember that I asked you to consider five key questions (*who, what, where, when* and *why*) and apply them to the topic that you had to discuss, thus allowing you to generate ideas as well as cover all the most important aspects. Let's now add two further questions (*what method* and *how*) and check how this works in practice. Imagine that you have been asked to write about a day out. Start by asking yourself the seven key questions:

  - **Who?** e.g. Who did you go with?
  - **What?** e.g. What did you do during the day out?
  - **Where?** e.g. Where did you go?
  - **When?** e.g. When did you go?
  - **Why?** e.g. Why did you go to this particular place?
  - **What method?** e.g. What means of transport did you use?
  - **How?** e.g. How did you find the day?

Writing short answers to these seven questions gives you an instant range of things you can write about. Sometimes you will find a particular question irrelevant or difficult to answer; in that case leave it out. (It may interest you to know that this method of covering all the aspects of a subject was devised by

Quintilian, a famous Roman writer.) When you have finished doing this, draw a line to separate your notes from the bottom half of the sheet.

- **Make up a plan.** Your next step is to look over your notes and think about how you are going to organise them. One simple way of doing this is to imagine that your piece of writing is in three stages: the beginning, the middle and the end. Draw three boxes on the bottom half of the sheet and label them *beginning, middle* and *end*. Then sort out your notes by placing them in the correct box, so that you have a rough structure that you can follow when you start to write. Once you have done this, you can either decide to commence writing or do some further work on shaping your notes into individual paragraphs; it all depends on how much time you have available and how complex the task is.

- **Start to write.** It's now time to write your first draft. Refer to the notes and plan you have just jotted down, and start writing. There are a few things to remember here: the first is that when you write an initial draft you don't necessarily have to start at the beginning of your plan and work through to the very end. Start off with the section that you feel most confident about and for which you have the most ideas; it doesn't matter if it is the beginning, middle or end. That way you will get off to a prompt start, and you'll be able to write most of the straightforward stuff without having to struggle over it—the difficult parts can wait till later!

There is another advantage to this; by tackling the easier parts first, you can build up the confidence that you will need for the more difficult sections. Think of it this way: when you start up a car from cold, the engine is less efficient and uses more fuel, so performance will not be so good. When the engine is fully warmed up, it's a different story: full efficiency, better fuel consumption and superior performance. Your brain is just like an engine; it needs some time to warm up, and it's not a good idea to overload it before it's in peak condition.

The second thing I suggest you do is use double spacing. If you are using lined paper, then write only on every second line—that way you'll have plenty of space to write in additional phrases and/or corrections at a future stage. If your paper is blank, then just leave a bit of space above each line. If you're using a word processor, set it to double-space your work automatically, then print out your first draft and amend it by hand.

The third thing to bear in mind when writing your first draft is to avoid checking your work too carefully. I advise my students at this point to put away their dictionaries and concentrate on writing what they know—there will be plenty time at a later stage to review and check their work thoroughly. The aim of drafting is to get down on paper as much as you can within a reasonable space of time, so don't worry about misspellings, shaky grammar, missed-out words or messy handwriting—after all, it is only meant to be a *first* draft and not the finished product. If you stop every two minutes to look up the dictionary you will lose momentum and it will become much harder to write.

One final piece of advice—at this stage try to avoid going into things in too much depth. Stick to the main points and areas you intend to cover. Remember that if you were an artist painting a picture you would have just completed your *sketch*; the *colour* and *detail* come later.

We now move on to the second phase, where you **REVIEW** the draft you have just written. Read it through carefully from beginning to end, resisting the temptation to look up words in the dictionary and/or check points of grammar. Then ask yourself if you have written enough; if you have been given a word limit, now is the time to check it. Don't laboriously count every single word you have written; find out the average number of words you have in a line, then multiply by the number of lines. (If you are working on the computer then your word processing program may have a word count feature.) If you haven't written enough, then use Quintilian to add extra detail; this can be done by going over the questions and imagining further areas about which you might write. Here is an example of what I mean, using the example of the day out essay I gave you earlier. As you will see, what I have done is to take the original seven questions and add on extra questions (these are in italics), the answers to which will provide the extra detail you require:

- **Who?** e.g. Who did you go with? *Why did you go with this particular person or persons? When did you ask them to go with you? What did they think of the day out?*

- **What?** e.g. What did you do during the day out? *Why did you do these particular activities? How long did you spend on each? Would you like to repeat them on a future occasion?*

- **Where?** e.g. Where did you go? *What is the place like? Where exactly is it located? Have you been there before?*

- **When?** e.g. When did you go? *How long did you spend there? Did you have enough time? When did you decide to return?*

- **Why?** e.g. Why did you go to this particular place? *What was the main reason for going there? Did it live up to expectations? Will you recommend it to others?*

- **What method?** e.g. What means of transport did you use? *How quickly did you arrive at your destination? How did you travel about during the day? How expensive was it?*

- **How?** e.g. How did you find the day? *Which aspect did you enjoy the most? Which part of the day did you least like? What did your companion(s) think?*

A couple of points to bear in mind: the first is that the amount of extra detail you add is totally up to you. I have added three extra questions to each original question; you could add more or less, or none at all. The second is that you may not want to add extra detail to all seven questions; it may be that you have already written quite a bit about *what* you did during the day out, so it would be unnecessary to add even more. The name of the game here is *flexibility*: during the review phase, you only add as much detail as you want to, and only in the places it is needed. Quintilian allows you to do this in a structured and precise way, so get into the habit of using the seven questions whenever you are faced with a piece of creative writing.

One final point: what happens if you write too much? The short answer is to be ruthless; cut your essay down until it is the required length. This can sometimes be difficult to do, but it's best done now while you are at the review stage. Remember that *quality* (rather than *quantity*) is what teachers are looking for when you write in the foreign language. By writing too much, you run the risk of increased error and lack of impact. So keep it short and snappy (but not too short) and you won't go far wrong.

The third phase is where we **AMEND** what we have written. This process involves checking the text for spelling and grammatical errors and correcting them. Most students find this phase really tiresome and often don't spend enough time on it. The result is that they submit work that is marred by frequent mistakes, many of which are avoidable. The more care and attention you spend on checking and amending, the more accurate your final essay will be. Teachers usually assess an essay by considering content, style and accuracy simultaneously as they read it, with their overall *impression* determining the final mark or grade. Your essay may be both imaginative and stylishly written, but if it is full of spelling and grammar mistakes then it will leave a negative impression on the reader, and may be downgraded. Most spelling and grammar mistakes can be avoided by following these pieces of advice:

- **Read it over.** The first step is to read over your draft with a view to spotting any *obvious* spelling and grammatical mistakes. By this I mean those errors that you can easily see and correct on the spot. Most of these will be slips of the pen, such as slight spelling mistakes that come about from working at speed. Correct these as you go along, and don't spend too much time on them; at this point there is no need to examine each piece of text in great detail, as we shall do this at the next stage.

- **Check the text.** Now it's time to take a much closer look at the accuracy of what you have written. There are several ways of doing this, but the one I recommend to my students is called **VEGAS.** (Unlike the city of the same name, it has nothing to do with gambling.) This is an easy way of remembering the four key areas of textual accuracy:

VErbs, Genders, Agreements, Spellings.

Working through **VEGAS** will ensure that you check through what you have written in the foreign language in a logical and systematic fashion, using your dictionary and grammar reference book or notes whenever appropriate. A word of caution: you have to work through *every* step of **VEGAS** for it to be completely effective. Many students start using it, but then give up halfway through, as they often find it time-consuming and tedious. All I can say is that writing well in the foreign language involves spending a fair amount of time on checking and amending your work; if you cut corners here, you can't expect to achieve the highest grades. So stick with it, even if you find the going hard—it will be worth it in the long run.

Let's begin with some advice on technique. One of the big problems students have when checking their work is missing errors that they would normally spot quite easily. Why does this happen? One reason is that when we have to check a large block of text, our eyes tend to race ahead of our brain, and we rush on to read the next phrase or sentence without giving ourselves enough time to think about what we have just read. This leads to a lot of mistakes being overlooked.

One solution to this problem is to take a ruler and place it on the line of text you are going to read over; this will prevent your eyes from wandering, as they will be guided automatically to the text in question. Then, as you read on, lower the ruler down to the next line, and so on until you complete your reading of the text. That way the text is always hidden from your eyes until you are ready to view it; when you do so, your gaze will be fully concentrated on the sentence or phrase in question, and it will be much easier to spot any errors.

It's now time to take a closer look at **VEGAS**. Let's begin with the first area: **VERBS**. I always tell my students that unless they know their verbs, their progress in learning a foreign language will be very limited. This is because the verb is the element around which the rest of a sentence is constructed—take away the verb, and you have no proper sentence. Mastery of the verb system in any language is the key to being able to express yourself effectively; if you don't know your verbs, then you will be unable to communicate. The first thing to do when checking any text you have written is to start at the beginning and work your way through every single verb, asking yourself the following questions:

- **Have I used the correct tense?** Think of what it is you are trying to say; are you referring to a present, past or future event? Or perhaps it's something you or someone else would like to do, i.e. the conditional.

- **Have I formed the verb correctly?** Check that you have formed the tense of the verb correctly. The verb may not follow the normal rules and may be *irregular,* in which case you have to be especially careful. Depending on the language and tense, some verbs may need an *auxiliary* or helping verb (usually the verbs *to have* and *to be*). Finally, the verb may need to *agree* with its subject. This can mean a couple of things: in the first instance, the part of the verb you use should match the subject of the sentence. If your subject is plural, then your verb has to be plural as well. In some languages the past participles of verbs also have to agree with the subject in *gender* as well as *number*. (Consult your teacher for further information on any of the concepts I have mentioned, as these differ considerably from language to language.)

We now move onto **GENDERS** and **AGREEMENTS**. Many languages assign genders to their nouns: in other words, a word might be masculine, feminine, or neuter. Knowing the correct gender of a noun is vital in many languages; for example, the words for *the* and/or *a* may change according to the gender of the noun to which they are attached. Alternatively adjectives describing a noun may have different forms for singular and plural, masculine and feminine; this is known by the term *agreements*. (We already mentioned this when we talked about verbs.) Find out if these concepts apply to the language you are learning and if they do, you should now go over your work a second time from beginning to end, checking all your nouns and adjectives for correct genders and agreements.

The third and last area in **VEGAS** is **SPELLINGS**. You should now read over your draft a final time, looking carefully for misspellings. (If you are fortunate enough to have typed your draft on a word processor and have a spell-check facility for your foreign language, then the computer will be able to do this for you.) Use your dictionary to double-check any doubtful spellings; this can be time-consuming but is well worthwhile. Here are a number of things to bear in mind when you are doing this:

- **Have you put in your accents?** Many foreign languages have accented letters, and these should always be written correctly as they are part of the correct spelling of the word. Make sure that you know which accents are used in your language and what their function is; after all, it's so much easier to remember to put them in if you know why they are there in the first place!

- **What about your plurals?** In many languages the plural of a noun will be spelled differently from the singular. Sometimes (as in English) it is a simple matter of adding an extra letter; other languages can be a little trickier. Make sure you know the rules for forming plurals and check those that you have written.

- **Watch out for words that resemble English.** One of the factors that help us learn a foreign language is the similarity of many words to their English equivalents (these words are known as *cognates*). This can be very convenient when we are trying to understand something, but can cause problems when we confuse the spelling of the foreign language word with its English counterpart. Get into the habit of checking carefully any such words, as it is all too easy to make mistakes here.

- **What about capitals and punctuation?** Some languages use capital letters for certain types of nouns. It is a good idea to check that you have done this if it applies to the language you are studying. Punctuation is also important; I like to tell my students that they should learn to *spell their sentences correctly*, and they can only do that by paying attention to their punctuation. A well-punctuated text is clearer to read and easier to understand, whatever language it is written in.

You have now worked your way through **VEGAS** and your text should now be fully checked. It's time to move on to the final phase, after which your work is done!

The fourth and last phase is perhaps the easiest: it is where you **WRITE** up the final version of your essay. Bear in mind that this will be the finished product that your teacher is going to see, so take care over it. Here are some things that you should be aware of when preparing your final version:

- **Take your time.** It's no use spending a lot of time on the first three phases only to rush the last one and make a lot of silly and avoidable mistakes. If you're copying out your final draft by hand, make sure that you copy accurately. If you're retyping parts of your final draft on the computer, watch out that you don't accidentally delete or change other parts of the text.

- **Take care over presentation.** Teachers are more inclined to look favourably on your work if it is tidy and well-presented. Make sure that your handwriting is neat and fully legible, otherwise you may have marks deducted. Consider using double-spacing; that way your teacher will have enough room to write comments or corrections above a particular word or phrase. If you are using a word processor, use one font only and make sure it is large enough. Good quality paper also makes a big difference. Remember also to put your name on your work and date it, especially if you intend doing further versions of the same piece in the future.

- **Read it over one last time.** Now that you've finally finished, don't be in a rush to get rid of it! It pays to have one final read before you hand it in to your teacher. I never cease to be amazed by how many extra mistakes I suddenly spot when I read my *final* version for a *final* time. Better late than never, I suppose.

Let's now remind ourselves of the *Four Phases of Effective Writing*:

- Write your first **DRAFT**.

- **REVIEW** what you have written.

- **AMEND** your text.

- **WRITE** your final version.

By this stage in the book you'll have noticed how fond I am of acronyms. This one is quite simple: **DRAW** (**D**raft, **R**eview, **A**mend, **W**rite). So to write well in the foreign language all you have to do is *draw*, and you don't even need to be artistic!

Work On Your Writing Skills

Writing well in the foreign language requires constant practice. In my opinion it is not enough to do only the written assignments that your teacher gives you—you have to take the initiative and go a little bit further. You can do this in a number of different ways, as outlined below:

- **Write regularly.** Try to get into the habit of writing something in the foreign language every day. It doesn't really matter how long or short, simple or complicated it is; the important thing is that you are putting pen to paper. For example, why not keep a simple diary in the foreign language? If you have read the chapter on speaking you will remember how I suggested keeping a daily audio-diary where you record three things: what you are doing at that precise moment, what you have done during the day and what you will be doing tomorrow. (This lets you practise the present, past and future tenses.) What I am now proposing is that you do exactly the same, but in a written form. Don't worry if you haven't yet covered all three tenses, as you can do a shorter version limiting yourself to one or two. A great idea would be to do both an audio *and* written diary that could be virtually identical; that way you practise both your speaking and writing skills on a daily basis. If you stick with this, eventually you will have quite a large amount of material that you can then read over and/or listen to at a later date—great for revision purposes.

  Another good way of making sure that you write regularly is to find someone to write to. This could be a pen-friend in the country whose language you are studying; if you have an e-mail link then daily communication is no problem. If you don't, then you will have to rely on traditional mail, which is obviously much slower. Corresponding with a native speaker is perhaps the best way to improve your writing (and reading) skills, as you can learn a lot from the replies you receive; not only do you get valuable reading comprehension practice, but you can include some of the new language you learn in your own writing.

  It may be, however, that you cannot find a native speaker to write to; in that case, why not correspond in the foreign language with another student in your class? This might seem a little artificial, but I can assure you that it works: what you do is write each other short notes or letters on a regular basis. You can also involve your teacher in the process by asking him or her to check what you both have written; that way you don't run the risk of repeating each other's errors.

- **Redraft your work.** If you were to ask me what was the single, most effective way of improving your writing skills, then this is it. Redrafting your pieces of writing on a regular basis ensures that you progress in your understanding of the foreign language and your ability to write it effectively. Why should this be so? In the first place very few of us can produce a piece of writing that is fault-free at the first attempt. There will always be an error or two, a paragraph that isn't as clear as it might be, a section that you could have made a little bit longer. Secondly, we all want to progress onto a higher level of writing expertise; a redraft gives us the opportunity to try out new vocabulary, expressions and constructions that will enrich our original. However, redrafting requires a structured and methodical approach, and for it to be fully effective you have to follow these steps:

  - **Re-read your work carefully**. This is important because it may be some time since you wrote your first version, and you will have to remind yourself of the content. Try to read with a critical eye, asking yourself these questions: *Why did I write that? How can I improve what I have written? What can I add or delete?* While you do this, note down any new ideas that come to you.

  - **Review and correct your mistakes**. The best time to redraft your work is obviously after it has been corrected by your teacher. All good teachers will tell you what grammatical and spelling mistakes you have made; go over all of these carefully and make sure that you do not repeat the same errors in your redraft. The best way of doing this is to make sure that you understand why you made the mistake in the first place—if you are in any doubt, consult your teacher. Remember that making mistakes and correcting them is all part of the learning process, so don't bury your head in the sand—face up to your errors, understand why you made them, and with a bit of luck they'll never bother you again. (You may also want to consider keeping an *error log*; see page 109 for more details of this.)

  - **Modify and add to your text**. This is what redrafting is all about—the chance to take something and re-create it. How far do you go? Obviously that depends on the original and the nature of its defects. Some of these may have already become apparent during your first re-reading and you may have already noted down some possible solutions. If your teacher has read the piece through then he or she may have made some comments about how it might be improved. These may fall into the following categories:

- **Too long or too short.** If your piece is too long, then review it and cut out any repetition, irrelevancy and excessive detail until you arrive at the required length. This can be a painful process but you have to be ruthless. Keep telling yourself that *less is more.* If your piece is too short, then you will have to consider how you can lengthen it. Try to use Quintilian to make sure that you have covered all aspects of a subject. Take care that you don't resort to needless repetition, long lists of things and going off on irrelevant tangents. These may well make your piece longer, but it'll probably end up a lot worse!

- **Lack of structure.** Many pieces of writing lack a clear overall structure. If your teacher has made this criticism of your work, start off by identifying the exact nature of the problem. The next step is to devise a new structure into which you will have to rearrange your ideas. (The most basic structure of all is the three-part one (*beginning, middle* and *end*) described on page 72.) Once you have done this, your piece should hang together a bit more effectively, but be warned: it may be difficult to put things right. The best solution may well be a fresh start, making sure that this time you think long and hard about *planning* your piece before you start to write it.

- **Level of language.** Your teacher may be concerned that the level of language you have used in your piece is not high enough. It may be written in a rather simplistic way and may not be a good reflection of what you actually know. Redrafting such a piece is a good opportunity to try to get your language onto a higher plane. Here are some tried and tested ways of doing this:

  - All good pieces of writing make use of what we might call *set phrases.* These are short phrases that you can use over and over again whatever you are writing, and are normally used to start off a sentence. Here are some examples that are useful if you are writing a *discursive* essay (i.e. one where you discuss a particular subject):

    I think that...I believe that...You have to...This allows me to...In my opinion...In the first place...On the contrary...In any case...To conclude...As for myself...In my opinion...In brief...After all...I find that...The aim is to...As for...That is because...It seems to me that...I tell myself that...The fact is that...The problem is that...To begin with...In other words...All I have to say is that...I'm convinced that...

(I could add many more, but by now you should have a clear idea of the kind of phrases I'm talking about.)

- Here is a second list that is more suited to *narrative* essays (i.e. those where you tell a story or describe an event):

Without hesitating...Without thinking...Without wasting any time...To my great surprise...To my great joy...To my great relief...Suddenly...Immediately...After doing this...Before doing this...Instead of doing that...Some time afterwards...Shortly afterwards...Five minutes later...Fortunately...Unfortunately...At that very moment...Eventually...Finally...

What you should do is make up your own lists and then try to use them at appropriate points in your writing. Remember that the point of these phrases is to make your text clearer, livelier and more readable, so try to get into the habit of using them regularly.

- Learn to *recycle* your best material. (You might think this is cheating, but I can assure you that it isn't!) What I am suggesting is that you look over your previous pieces of work and pick out those parts of them that you can use again, even if you have to change them to fit the new context. For example, you may have earned the praise of your teacher by using a particular grammar construction really well in your last essay; why not include it in your new piece of work? Or there may be some new vocabulary and expressions from a previous assignment that deserve to be used again. In this way you will be revising and practising language with which you are familiar, but adapting it to new situations.

- As the saying goes, *Imitation is the sincerest flattery.* One of the most effective strategies for learning to write well is to look at what others have done, and then try to imitate it. The best way of doing this is to make the most of your reading opportunities in the foreign language. Look at how authors write: how they construct sentences, how they use tenses, and the type of vocabulary they choose. Then try to imitate them in your own writing, without necessarily copying word for word. All good teachers tend to analyse texts when they practise reading comprehension skills, so pay attention to the explanations they give—understanding how an author puts across his or her message is vital if you wish to write a similar message. One last thing: please imitate your teacher. There will be times when he or she will write creatively for the entire class, for example by scripting a model answer for a particular essay title. When this happens, make the most of it and encourage your teacher to do it much more often!

The Final Word

During the course of this chapter I have given you a great deal of advice about writing in the foreign language. There are only a few things I have left to say, so here they are:

- Try not to think in English when you write in the foreign language, as word for word translations are rarely correct.

- Don't run before you can walk. Trying to be over-ambitious will increase your chances of error. Use only language with which you feel comfortable and are confident about using accurately. But remember that you do have to take the occasional risk if you are to progress to a higher level.

- Every good piece of writing should have *Something new, something old, something borrowed, something bold.* This is my version of a well-known rhyme about weddings, and here is what it means:

  - *Something new*: new and original material that you are confident about using.

  - *Something old*: recycled and modified material from earlier pieces of work.

  - *Something borrowed*: material from other authors that you have imitated.

  - *Something bold*: material that breaks new ground for you (and that you might not be entirely sure about), taking you onto a higher level of language. Caution: use sparingly!

The very last word comes from the English author Samuel Johnson: *What is written without effort is in general read without pleasure.* You have been warned!

PART III
Going It Alone

Using Your Textbook

Most students who learn a foreign language in a classroom situation do so from a textbook. This is normally chosen by your teacher and may be part of a larger course stretching over a number of years. A few teachers prefer not to have a textbook at all, and produce their own materials for use in class. The general pattern, however, is for the class to work primarily from a textbook, with additional materials being provided by the teacher if and when required—these might be supplementary books, worksheets, extra texts, etc.

Most teachers will work their way systematically through a textbook, with others taking a more selective approach. Whatever system your teacher has of working, bear in mind that your textbook can be your best friend, but only if you treat it properly and use it effectively. The purpose of this chapter is to show you how to do this, and to prove to you that your textbook is probably the single most valuable resource you have.

Textbook Basics

- **Take care of your textbook.** This is especially important if you have been given it on loan—remember that a future student will have to use it after you, so make sure that it is returned to your teacher in good condition as it may be expensive to replace. Many students cover their textbooks to ensure that they are protected against minor damage, but check first with your teacher that this is permitted. If you are able to, consider buying your own copy—that way you'll able to pencil your own notes in the margins as you go along.

- **Keep it in an accessible place.** Your textbook is of no use to you if you cannot find it easily every time you need it. Try to find a convenient location for it and return it there once you have finished with it. (You may think that I am stating the obvious here, but being well organised definitely pays off. Time spent searching for your textbook is time you could have devoted to your studies.)

- **Bring it along to your classes.** You won't get the best out of your classes unless you bring your textbook. If you forget to do this you disadvantage yourself and others, since you will probably have to share a textbook with another student (making it difficult for either of you to concentrate fully).

- **Make sure that your name and address are on it.** I recall once lending an Italian textbook to a student who never returned it. Ten years later I received it in the post, together with a note from a lady who said she had found it on a seat as she was getting off a flight to Italy. How did she know it was mine? Simple: I had put my name and school address on the inside cover.

Get to Know Your Textbook

I once remember reading that we only use about 2% of our brains. The same thing could be said about the way we use textbooks. Many students never explore the full potential of what is their most useful asset. This is because they never take the time to get to know their textbook thoroughly, and so are unable to use it effectively. Most foreign language textbooks offer a wide variety of resources presented in an accessible and user-friendly format, so there is really no excuse for not being able to find your way around. What I propose to do now is to give you a short tour of the average foreign language textbook. Read this over carefully, and then have another look at your own textbook. You'll be surprised at what you might find!

Anatomy of a Textbook

The main purpose of a textbook is to present you with a structured and self-contained learning experience in the foreign language (this is why they are often described as *courses* or *coursebooks*). Most textbooks start off from one particular stage in your language learning and take you forward to a higher level. They do this by providing you with a balanced mixture of listening, speaking, reading and writing activities linked to presentations of new vocabulary and grammar explanations. This means that you are supposed to work through them from cover to cover, as each chapter or unit will build on the skills and knowledge you have learned at the previous stage. Some textbooks are part of a series that is meant to encompass several years' work, while others are self-contained; check your own to see what type it is. Once you have done this, you can look over these common features of many current foreign language textbooks:

- **The introduction or preface.** This will normally tell you who the textbook is aimed at, as well as giving you some information about the layout and how to access the various parts. It is best read before you start using a textbook for the first time.

- **The list of contents.** This is usually placed at the beginning. Get into the habit of using it, as it will allow you to find quickly what you are looking for. It also gives a useful overview of all the areas covered by the textbook.

- **Individual chapters or units.** Most textbooks are divided into chapters or units, each of which will be similar in layout. The most common model is a language presentation followed by exercises covering the four basic skills, along with some of the additional features itemised below. Many textbooks deal with language on a *topical* basis, so you may find that each chapter or unit covers a different vocabulary topic or sector. Here is a list of the most important topic areas:

  - **Personal Information**, e.g. name, age, birthday, star sign, appearance, personality, likes and dislikes, future aspirations, family members, family relationships, friends, pets, daily routine, etc.

  - **Home and Local Area,** e.g. where you live, description of house, rooms, furniture and fittings, garden, household chores, sights and facilities in local area, environmental issues, etc.

  - **Travel and Transport,** e.g. travel by car, train, plane, boat, etc.; booking tickets, making travel enquiries and reservations, public transport issues, etc.

  - **School, College and University,** e.g. place of study, subjects studied, teaching staff, facilities, timetables, examinations, homework, qualifications, etc.

  - **Work,** e.g. jobs, occupations, careers, posts, places of work, conditions of service, working day, etc.

  - **Food and Drink,** e.g. types of food and drink, cafés, restaurants, mealtimes, diets, nutrition, healthy eating, etc.

  - **Shopping and Services,** e.g. shops, banks, post offices, weights and measures, sizes, quantities, prices, etc.

  - **Leisure Time,** e.g. hobbies, pastimes, sports, television, cinema, etc.

  - **Holidays,** e.g. destinations, activities, sightseeing, accommodation, weather, etc.

- **Accidents, Illnesses and Emergencies,** e.g. aches and pains, doctors, hospitals, injuries, mishaps, catastrophes, etc.

- **The Wider World,** e.g. society, politics, religion, social issues, lifestyles, etc.

As you can see, the topic areas I have outlined above are quite wide-ranging, and it may be that your textbook subdivides them even further. It is also true to say that the further you advance in your language studies, the more you will be expected to express your own views and opinions. Furthermore, you might be excused for thinking that the above topic areas cover *all human life*—and you would be right! Studying a foreign language involves, by its very nature, acquainting oneself with most aspects of human existence and not with a small, limited body of knowledge.

- **Learning outcomes.** The beginning of each chapter or unit may have a list of what are called *learning outcomes*. This is basically a checklist of all the things you will cover during your study of the chapter or unit. Get into the habit of referring to it before you start, as it is always a good idea to know exactly what you are working towards. Look back at the learning outcomes at regular intervals, both to reassure yourself that you are on course and to remind yourself of what is coming up. Then, once you have completed the chapter or unit, you can review the learning outcomes and tick off the ones you have achieved. Doing this can increase your motivation, as well as give you a clear idea of your strengths and weaknesses. It also tells you what you have to revise before you progress to the next unit or chapter. Finally, learning outcomes provide a yardstick to check if your teacher is covering all aspects of the course. Many teachers make a point of going over learning outcomes with students before commencing the unit or chapter, and will review them at the end. If they don't, make sure you do!

- **Vocabulary lists.** There will usually be a presentation of new vocabulary and idioms at some point in the chapter or unit. This is usually linked to the topic area(s) being covered.

- **Grammar explanations and exercises.** Textbooks often vary in the way in which they deal with grammar. Some prefer to present any relevant grammar points (together with practice exercises) during the course of individual chapters or units, whereas others have a grammar reference section at the end of the book. (This may also include tables of regular and irregular verbs in a variety of different tenses.)

- **Revision sections.** Parts of your textbook may be devoted to revising things you have learned earlier. Sometimes these are placed after every three or four chapters or units, or alternatively they may be grouped at the end of the book.

- **Background knowledge.** Learning a foreign language involves increasing your knowledge of the country, its inhabitants, its customs, its culture and its history. All good textbooks will present this information either in a separate English section or by integrating it with the language presentation. Unfortunately many students tend to neglect this area of language learning, which is a pity as good background knowledge can be a positive asset. Let me put it this way: the more you know about the country, its culture and the lifestyle of its inhabitants, then the more able you will be to cope with its language.

- **Classroom language.** In recent years there has been a great increase in the amount of foreign language used within the classroom. This involves both teachers and students using the foreign language to conduct the business of the class; examples might include classroom commands, requests, instructions, reprimands, etc. Using the foreign language in the classroom at every available opportunity is a powerful stimulus to learning. Many textbooks recognise its importance and include a collection of the most common and useful classroom phrases. It's well worth taking a look at these and trying some out in class—you will both impress your teacher and increase your confidence in the spoken language.

- **Glossaries.** Nearly every textbook has a glossary at its end. This is basically a mini-dictionary that lists, in alphabetical order, all the main vocabulary items that have occurred in the course of the book. Glossaries are a handy alternative to using a dictionary, as they are both quicker to use (because of the reduced number of words and expressions) and more convenient (all you do is flick through the back of the book).

- **Index.** Finally, we come to the index. In foreign language textbooks this is normally placed after the glossary, and lists page numbers for such things as vocabulary topics and grammar points. Learn to use the index whenever you need to find the location of these items; it is far quicker than wading through whole sections of the book hoping to spot what you are looking for.

Use Your Textbook Effectively

It's no use knowing your textbook inside out if you are not going to put that knowledge to good use. Here are some ways of doing just that:

- **Keep one step ahead.** Once you are familiar with the layout of your textbook, you will be able to see exactly how your teacher uses it in class. This can be valuable because most teachers tend to approach each unit of work in much the same way, following a fixed sequence with which you will soon become familiar. Knowing what your teacher is likely to do next from your textbook means that you can look over this work before it is done in class. That way you will be more prepared for the lesson and will derive greater benefit from it. As the saying goes, *forewarned is forearmed*; anticipating what is to be taught makes the learning of it all the easier.

- **Refer to your textbook as you work.** The function of your textbook is not only to teach you new language, but also to act as a reference book. As I have described above, most textbooks have vocabulary lists (often arranged by topics), grammar explanations, verb tables, background knowledge sections, a glossary and an index. Get into the habit of using these regularly as you work, as they can help you in all sorts of ways. Here is an example: imagine you have to write an essay on food and drink. First of all you might have a look at the background knowledge sections to see if there is any information on eating and drinking habits; then you could refer to the food and drink vocabulary list to gather together all the words and expressions you will need. Once you start writing you will want to do several things: check your verbs, get information on a particular grammar point, and look up words. Your textbook can help you with much of this as long as you know *where* to look for the information you require. If you can't remember, then use the list of contents or the index; that's what they're there for!

- **Bookmark your most important pages.** There may be one or more sections in your textbook that you refer to constantly, such as the grammar reference section, verb tables, vocabulary lists, etc. You can waste a lot of time constantly thumbing through your textbook looking for these pages. One solution to this problem is to use sticky notes as temporary bookmarks. Label them and then place them towards the edge of the side or top of the page, so that they stick out enough for you to catch hold of them. If you want, you can use different colours of sticky notes—one colour for grammar, another for verbs, and so on. Eventually they will get a little tatty and will start to peel off, but replacing them takes only a minute.

- **Take notes from your textbook.** It is a good idea to have a notebook into which you can copy the main points of the work you have been doing from your textbook. The two principal areas you might include are grammatical constructions and vocabulary. I tell my students to divide their notebooks into two: grammar at the front, vocabulary at the back. That way, the two areas are kept separate and are more easily accessed. There are several advantages in keeping a notebook; the first is that the very act of copying things in a structured and systematic fashion can help you to learn and internalise new vocabulary and structures. The second is that your notebook becomes a record of your own personal achievement in language learning; what it contains is what you know and have learnt, and as such it can become a handy tool for revision purposes. The third is to do with the fact that you may not own your own textbook, and are using a copy lent to you by your place of learning. You will therefore have to return it at some point. In this case, keeping a notebook is a great way of ensuring that you still have access to all that you have learnt, long after your textbook has been handed back.

- **Use your textbook to revise.** As I stated earlier, many textbooks have revision sections. Your teacher may already be including them in his or her schedule of work, but if not try to go over them yourself. Learning a language effectively depends to a great extent on our willingness to revise what we have already done. The revision sections in many textbooks offer a convenient, comprehensive and structured way of doing just that.

- **Explore any extra resources.** Your textbook is not just a book—it is much more! Many textbooks have extra resources that can be used effectively by students; all you have to do is find out about them, as sometimes they are only made available to the teacher. Here is a list of some of the things you should ask about:

  - Tapes and CD's of listening materials.
  - Workbooks.
  - Software.
  - Worksheets.
  - Assessment materials.
  - Publisher or textbook website.

Most teachers will be happy to give you information on these extra resources and how best you can use them. A word of advice: if you borrow anything, be sure to return it as soon as you have finished with it—that way it can be made available for use by another student.

The Final Word

Francis Bacon once said that *some books are to be tasted, others to be swallowed, and some few to be chewed and digested*. What about textbooks? As a languages teacher I would have to say three things:

1. *Tasting* a textbook will give you only the flavour and not the nourishment.

2. *Swallowing* a textbook will choke you.

3. *Chewing and digesting* a textbook will ensure that you absorb all its goodness.

What's it going to be? I think you know the answer to that one!

Using a Dictionary

Apart from your textbook, your dictionary is perhaps the most valuable resource that you can have when learning a foreign language. Having said that, learning to use a dictionary properly is not as easy as it might appear, and much of this chapter will be devoted to giving you clear advice on how to use one effectively.

Before we get onto that, however, it might be useful to have a look at the kind of dictionaries available and how you should go about choosing one. This assumes, of course, that you do require a dictionary at this point in your language learning—if you have just started, for example, you may find that the glossary at the back of your textbook is more than sufficient for your purposes. If so, then it makes precious little sense to invest in a massive dictionary—it's a bit like using a sledgehammer to crack a nut.

If, however, you are already well down the route of learning a language, then buying your own dictionary makes a lot of sense. You'll notice that I am suggesting that you *buy* your own copy rather than use a dictionary provided for you by your place of learning. There are several good reasons for doing this. In the first place, you may not be permitted to take dictionaries home with you—not much use if you have homework to do! Your place of learning dictionary may also be a little worse for wear, and may be missing the odd page (always the very page you need to look up a word). It may also be too big or too small for your needs, or a little out of date and not particularly user-friendly. Getting your own dictionary means that you will have none of these problems, and you'll save a lot of time and effort into the bargain.

Choosing a Dictionary

Think of what it would be like to do an advanced mathematics course without a calculator—you might be able to manage it, but it would probably take much more time and effort. Could you do an equivalent course in a foreign language without a dictionary? Not so easy—if you don't know a word or expression, then looking it up in a dictionary is usually your only option.

Like calculators, dictionaries come in all shapes and sizes, and you have to make sure that you find one that is suited to your requirements. In a moment I'll look at some of the things that you have to consider when buying a dictionary, but first of all I would like to point out that there are two basic types of dictionary: those that translate from English to the foreign language (and vice versa) and those which give definitions in the foreign language of foreign language words and expressions (i.e. the equivalent of an English dictionary, but all in the foreign language). This second type is only of use if you are a fairly advanced learner, so I'll assume that you are interested in buying the first type. Here are some factors that you should take into consideration:

- **Purpose.** Think carefully about the stage that you are at in your language learning, as this will determine what kind of dictionary you require. It's no use buying a very large dictionary if you are doing a short beginner's course and don't intend to continue any further. On the other hand, it would be foolish to buy a small dictionary only to find that it does not contain enough words and expressions to deal with the kind of work you are doing. The trick with buying dictionaries is to think ahead. If you are going to be studying a foreign language for the next few years, then it's better to invest in a dictionary that will support you when you reach a more advanced stage, rather than have to upgrade along the way. What I suggest you do is get some advice about what you should choose. Your teacher may be able to recommend a particular dictionary and show or lend you a copy of it—that way you can try before you buy!

- **Size.** The larger the dictionary, the more words and expressions it will contain, making it more likely that you will find what you are looking for. Larger dictionaries always give examples of words and expressions being used in their proper context; this makes it much easier for the language learner to understand and imitate them. The downside is this: when you use a large dictionary it takes you longer to look up words since there are more pages to flick through. You also run the risk of losing your way as you battle through countless different uses of a word before finding the one you're looking for. You also have to take into account portability. It's no use buying a six-volume monster if you have to carry it to your place of learning each day. If you can afford it, then the best solution might be to buy a reasonably-sized dictionary for use only at home, together with a smaller and lighter version for use at your place of learning. That way you get the best of both worlds.

- **Durability.** How long is your dictionary going to last before it starts to fall apart? Obviously this depends to some extent on how often you carry it around with you—as we all know, books that travel with their owners suffer a fair bit of wear and tear. Make sure you have a good look at the binding; if it's sewn, then it should last a reasonable amount of time, but if it's glued, then you might find that the pages will eventually become loose. (A dictionary with missing pages is about as useful as a pen with no ink.) Examine the cover; is it hardback or paperback? Hard-backed dictionaries will obviously last a lot longer, but you will find that some publishers are now offering dictionaries with soft, flexible, laminated covers—these are also quite durable. As with most things in life you get what you pay for, so it's a good idea to wait that little bit longer until you can afford a superior quality dictionary—it will be worth it in the long run.

- **Date of last revision.** Find out when the dictionary was last revised before you buy it: the more recent it is, the better. Many of the cheaper, paperback dictionaries are reprints of older dictionaries and may not contain up-to-date language. This can be a problem when you attempt to look up words and expressions that have recently entered the language. If you don't believe me, try looking up *DVD player* in a twenty year-old dictionary!

- **Format.** Have a look at the way the dictionary is laid out. How large is the type? Is it quite easy to read? Many dictionaries use colour coding to differentiate between the various sections or to highlight key words within an entry—check that the dictionary you are looking at uses this, as it makes it much easier to find your way about. Some dictionaries use thumbnails so that you can easily locate a particular letter section without having to flick through the pages. (One of the first dictionaries I ever bought had these and they saved me a great deal of time.) Remember also that first impressions are lasting impressions; opening a dictionary for the first time will tell you how user-friendly it is likely to be. If it looks good and feels right, then you will probably enjoy using it. If not, then look elsewhere. You have to be comfortable with a dictionary, otherwise you'll find excuses for not using it.

- **Extra sections.** It used to be that a dictionary served one purpose only: to offer translations from English into the foreign language, and vice versa. Not any more! Modern dictionaries have a number of extra sections that can give you help with a whole series of language items. Here are some of the things on offer: regular and irregular verb tables, information on tenses, grammar points, numbers, time expressions, question words, countries and nationalities, letter phrases, maps, advice on effective dictionary use, business vocabulary, common abbreviations, essay phrases—the list is endless. Obviously it is the bigger dictionaries that offer the most features, but even smaller ones are now packed with a surprising amount of extra information. So when you choose a dictionary have a close look at these additional sections. Ask yourself how many of them are relevant to your needs—sometimes there will be sections that you will never use. I recommend to my own students that they look first of all for a good regular and irregular verb section, complete with some explanation of tenses. In my experience this is by far the most useful extra to have, especially when you are using the dictionary in an examination situation.

- **Quality of entries.** This is the acid test of how good a dictionary really is. Imagine you are going to buy a car. You might like the styling, be able to afford the purchase price, be impressed by how it's put together, and admire all the extra equipment fitted to it. You may even have read positive reviews about its performance and reliability. But unless you take a test drive, you're never going to be totally sure about what you're buying. Dictionaries are very similar—you have to try them out for yourself. Here are a few suggestions about how best to do this:

  - **How many examples does it offer for each entry?** To check this out look up a few English words that can have more than one meaning or that occur in different contexts. Here's an example of what I mean: the verb *to drop* can be used in a number of different ways. We can talk about *dropping something on the floor, dropping a subject at school, dropping someone off at the station, dropping off to sleep*; if we are tired of hearing someone talk about something then we tell them to *drop it*. Any dictionary worth its salt will clearly set out all these different uses and provide you with examples of them in the foreign language.

  - **How good is the pronunciation guide?** Some of the larger dictionaries claim to show you how to pronounce words. They do this by spelling them *phonetically*, i.e. spelling them not as they are written but as they are said. (Words are normally rewritten using the International Phonetic Alphabet; an explanation of this system is usually included in the dictionary.) But, as the saying goes, the proof is in the pudding. Look up a few words that you know how to pronounce perfectly and check out how effective the system is.

  - **How abbreviated are the abbreviations?** Many dictionaries can be quite awkward and irritating to use, because you constantly have to look up what the abbreviations mean. Some recent dictionaries avoid this by abandoning abbreviations altogether, so that instead of *prep.* you have *preposition*. It may take up more space, but it is certainly a lot friendlier!

So that's it. You've checked out the various options available using the advice I've given you above, you've gone to your local bookstore, handed over your hard-earned money and are now the proud owner of a shiny, new dictionary. All you have to do now is to learn how to use it!

Using a Dictionary Effectively

Being able to use a dictionary quickly and effectively is vital when learning a foreign language. Like all skills, it is something that you have to practise actively; if you neglect to do this, then you will never get the most out of what your dictionary has to offer. You will also find that it takes you much longer to find the word or expression that you are looking for—and time (as we know) can be precious, especially in an examination situation.

The first step towards effective dictionary use is to remind yourself of the basic features of any bilingual dictionary. These sometimes vary a little according to which dictionary you are using, but are fundamentally the same as regards their position and function:

- **Two halves make a whole.** All bilingual dictionaries are split into two halves: the first half will list all the foreign language words followed by their English translations, whereas the second half will list all the English words followed by their foreign language translations. So if you are using a French-English dictionary, for example, you would look up French words in the first half to find their English equivalents. If you are working the other way around (i.e. from English to French) then you use the second half.

- **Know your ABC.** Words are always listed in alphabetical order in both halves of the dictionary—this makes them relatively easy to find (provided we know the alphabet!). Most dictionaries also print *guide words* in the top corner of each page. The guide word on the left-hand page will be the same as the first entry on that page, whereas the guide word on the right-hand page will be the last entry on that page. Guide words are almost always printed in bold characters or in colour so that the eye is drawn to them; you can therefore see at a glance whether the word you are looking for is going to be on that particular page.

- **Headwords.** A *headword* is quite simply the first word in an entry. It will be printed in bold characters or in colour to allow it to stand out from the rest of the entry. It is the first word that you look up.

- **What's in an entry?** When you read the entry that follows a headword you may find the following information:

- **The grammatical status of the headword.** This tells you if the word is a noun, verb, adjective, preposition, etc.; in the case of nouns the gender may also be given.

- **How to pronounce it.** The headword may be spelt phonetically (see above for an explanation).

- **A translation of the headword.** A translation of the headword will now be given. Some words with more than one meaning may have a different translation for each meaning; make sure that you look at the correct translation, otherwise you could end up saying something totally unexpected. I remember one of my students translating the following sentence into French: *There was a tap on the door.* Not knowing the word for *tap* she reached for her dictionary and wrote down the first translation she saw: *un robinet.* As those of you who know some French will have realised, what she actually wrote down was that there was a *tap* (i.e. the type that you use to turn water on and off) *on the door*, a strange sight indeed! So be careful when you see more than one translation of the headword listed, as it's easy to make mistakes. Most good dictionaries will clearly list and explain all possible translations of the headword; all you have to do is make sure that you read these carefully.

- **Examples of the headword being used.** All dictionaries try to give examples of a particular headword being used in its various contexts. These examples are valuable as they show you the headword as it is actively used in the language; if you're lucky you'll then find the exact translation that you're looking for, and if not you can always modify it to suit your own purposes. Let's illustrate this by looking at a typical entry in a French to English dictionary. If we look up the English headword *service* in the English to French section we might find that six different contexts are listed, with one or more examples being given for each context. The entry may look something like this:

SERVICE *(noun) 1. (bus, train);* **le service**; le service des autobus est assez lent le weekend *the bus service is quite slow at weekends; 2. (military);* **le service militaire**; il doit faire son service militaire *he has to do his military service; 3. (in a restaurant);* **le service**; le service est compris *service is included; 4. (emergency);* **les services des urgences**; les services des urgences sont arrivés après cinq minutes *the emergency services arrived after five minutes; 5. (church);* **un office**; il y a un office à onze heures le dimanche *there is a church service at eleven on Sundays; 6. (cars);* **une révision**; ma voiture a besoin d'une révision complète *my car needs a complete service.*

As you can see, the English word *service* can be used in a number of different ways, and the translation into the foreign language can vary accordingly—so we have *un office* for a church service and *une révision* for a car service. Bear in mind, however, that the above entry is only given as an illustration; your own dictionary may list many more contexts and examples, or it may well have less—it all depends on its size. What you have to do is make sure that you read through them all carefully until you find what you are looking for.

- **Style and Register.** Dictionaries don't just offer you translations; they also give you advice on the linguistic status of words and expressions. These are sometimes called *style and register labels*, and here are some of the most common:

  - **Abbreviation.** This tells you that the word is a short form of a longer original (e.g. *fridge* instead of *refrigerator*).

  - **Archaic.** This means that the word or expression is out of date and no longer in common use in the language.

  - **Dialect.** This indicates that the word or expression is only used in one particular part of the country.

  - **Diminutive.** This applies to words that indicate smaller or lesser versions of something (e.g. *kitchenette* instead of *kitchen*).

  - **Euphemism.** This is when a word or expression is a more gentle or sensitive way of describing something that is harsh or unpleasant (e.g. *to pass away* instead of *to die*).

  - **Exclamation.** Used to describe words or expressions that are said in a sharp or sudden way, often with some emotion.

  - **Informal.** This means that the word or expression is slang and should only be used in appropriate circumstances.

  - **Vulgar.** No need to explain this one—avoid these words and expressions at all costs!

There are, of course, many other style and register labels that you will gradually get to know the more you use the dictionary.

So that's it. We have reviewed the basic features of a bilingual dictionary and are ready to consider how effectively we can use it. I'm going to start by saying something that may seem to be contradictory: *the best way of using a dictionary is to avoid using it too often.* Let me explain myself: overuse of the dictionary is, in my experience, one of the most common faults we make when learning a foreign language.

For example, many students panic when they encounter new words and expressions in a foreign language text. The reflex action in such situations is to reach for the dictionary and start looking up everything in sight. Some students even look up words and expressions that they already know, just to reassure themselves that they are on the right track. This is fine if you have all the time in the world, but most of us are working against the clock, either in an examination situation or under the usual pressure to meet deadlines.

It's much better to take a more reasoned and analytical approach. What you have to learn to do is *think*; look carefully at the word or expression and try to work out the meaning, using the *Triple S* test I have described on pages 60–61. This will often work, and you will find that you save considerable time and effort. If it doesn't, then it's time to reach for the dictionary. As I have said above, looking up words and expressions is all the easier if you know the layout of your dictionary and how individual entries are organised, so spend a lot of time acquainting yourself with this. The final step is then to ensure that you get plenty practice using your dictionary.

Practice Makes Perfect

How can you best practise dictionary skills? Here are some suggestions:

- **Find the right letter.** Being able to look up words and expressions in the shortest possible time is a basic skill that you should try to develop. Students often waste a lot of time finding the proper part of the dictionary from which to start their search. It's easy enough to distinguish between the two main sections (English to the foreign language and the foreign language to English) as these conveniently divide the dictionary into two equal parts. They will often be separated by a coloured section in the middle (perhaps containing verb tables or useful expressions) so that you can see at a glance which half to open. However, the problem is trying to find the alphabetical sections.

Let's say, for example, that you want to look up an English word beginning with the letter *G*. Step one takes very little time; you open the dictionary at random somewhere in the English to foreign language section. Who knows, you may be lucky and open at the *G*'s, in which case all you have to do is flick through a few pages until you find your word. What usually happens is that you open at another letter, and then have to rummage through quite a few pages until you find the *G*'s.

Some dictionaries (but not enough, in my opinion) get round this problem by using a system called *thumbnails*. These are small indentations on the sides of the pages that are labelled with all the different letters. All you do is place your finger in one and the dictionary will open at the correct section.

If you don't have thumbnails, then there is an alternative system that you can try. Get some small sticky notes, label them with the letters of the alphabet, and position them at the edges of the pages in your dictionary so that they jut out slightly. That way you'll be able to see instantly which part of the dictionary you should open to access a particular letter. (What I am describing is the equivalent of the sets of tabbed dividers you can buy to separate sections of a loose-leaf folder.) This should speed up things considerably, and after a while you could even remove the sticky notes and rely on your own visual judgement.

- **Speed tests.** The next step after you practise finding the correct letter is to see how fast you can find individual words. One way of doing this is to set yourself a series of speed tests. This is how it works: first of all you decide how many words you are going to look up. Let's say that you go for five in English and another five in the foreign language. Then choose the words themselves and write them down one after the other, in any order you like. (It doesn't really matter which words you go for, as long as they all begin with a variety of different letters.) Then get a clock or watch with a second hand (or a stopwatch if you have one) ready alongside your dictionary. What you then have to do is look up the ten words as fast as you can, writing down the precise time it takes you to do this.

After that it's a case of trying to better your time by looking up the same ten words again and again. This can be a little tedious, but you could introduce an element of competition by having a race with your fellow students. In this case, get a neutral to choose ten words that it's unlikely anyone knows; the winner will be the person who writes down the ten meanings in the shortest time. (Make sure, however, that everyone is using the same dictionary!)

If you practise these speed tests on a regular basis you will find that the average time it takes you to look up a word will drop considerably. Getting this average as low as you can will give you a significant performance advantage in examinations, as well as making you a more efficient language learner.

- **Dictionary skills packs.** If you feel that you need some really intensive practice, then one solution is to work through a *dictionary skills pack*. These include a range of exercises that are specifically designed for the foreign language you are studying. These packs are not usually on sale in normal bookshops, but are supplied directly by educational publishers to educational institutions (often in the form of photocopy masters); if you are interested contact your teacher. Many language departments also offer short courses on dictionary skills (sometimes these are integrated into normal coursework); if there is nothing available, then it's time to suggest the idea to your teacher.

The Final Word

There are just a couple of things left to talk about. The first involves alternatives to the traditional form of dictionary (i.e. a book). There are two of these: computer and Internet-based programmes, and electronic handheld translators (information on the first is given on pages 131–132).

Many students ask me for my opinion on electronic handheld translators; what I tell them is that at the present time they are really no proper substitute for a book-based dictionary. This is because they tend to give translations of headwords only, and don't always give detailed explanations or examples of usage. That's fine if you're walking around the foreign country and need to know a particular word in a hurry; you just reach into your pocket, pull out your translator, key in the word and up it will come. Great—but when you try to use it when tackling a reading comprehension exercise or essay, you'll find that it isn't sufficiently detailed. Of course, technology is advancing all the time and it may be that in the not too distant future these electronic dictionaries will take over completely—we'll just have to wait and see. One final point to bear in mind: if you do buy one, check that you will be able to use it during public examinations, as sometimes the use of electronic aids is not permitted.

The second and last thing I want to mention is *reading*. What, you may ask, does this have to do with dictionary use? Let me explain. Students who read constantly, either in English or in the foreign language, tend to make the best use of dictionaries. This is because reading is the best way of building up what I like to call *word power*. This is not only getting to know new words and expressions, but also being able to use them flexibly and creatively. The result is that when you look up a word in a foreign language dictionary, you are better equipped to understand what the entry is telling you. So my advice to you is to get out there and read as much as possible—the higher your word power, the more you will get out of the dictionary, and the less often you will have to use it!

Doing Homework

Learning a foreign language doesn't just happen in the classroom. There are some aspects of language learning that teachers find more convenient to address by setting homework, whereas others are best done during class time. For example, it is normally easier to practise speaking in class rather than at home, where you might have nobody to talk to. Grammar explanations and language presentations are also best done by the teacher, as you have the chance to ask questions about any difficulties you might be having. Listening practice is also predominantly done in the classroom, as the sources (CD's, tapes, the foreign language assistant) are not always available to the student at home.

However, there remain quite a few areas that teachers tend to practise and consolidate through the setting of homework tasks: the most important of these are reading comprehension exercises, essay work and vocabulary learning. But what, you may wonder, is the purpose of homework in the languages classroom? This might seem a rather pointless question, but I think it is important that we are clear about just why teachers set homework to languages students. Here are some reasons that spring immediately to mind:

- Homework allows us the chance to reflect on, learn, practise and revise what we have learned in class.

- If given regularly, it encourages us to work continuously on improving our language skills.

- It teaches us to work independently and efficiently through managing our time effectively.

- It plugs the gaps left by normal classroom teaching.

- When corrected regularly by the teacher, it gives us a good idea of our strengths and weaknesses and shows us what we have to do to improve

- When done well, it gives us a sense of attainment and worth, and spurs us on to greater effort.

- It serves as a record of achievement in our learning of the foreign language.

Reading over all these excellent reasons for doing homework should convince you that it is not something to be taken lightly or even neglected. Yet that is precisely what many students do, with the result that their progress in the foreign language is severely limited. The purpose of this chapter is not only to demonstrate the importance of homework in learning a foreign language, but also to point out some ways in which you can make the most of it. To do this we first have to look at the various types of foreign language homework set by teachers.

Types of Homework

There are three main types of homework assignments given by foreign language teachers:

- **Formal homework.** This is any type of written or recorded homework that the teacher takes in and corrects personally. Examples of formal homework might include taped speaking assignments, reading comprehension exercises and essays. Marks or grades for this type of homework are normally noted by the teacher.

- **Informal homework.** This is identical to the above, with the major difference being that it is not assessed individually by the teacher, but is corrected as a whole-class activity by the students themselves. Marks or grades for this type of homework are not usually recorded by the teacher.

- **Learning homework.** This type of homework is when the teacher gives the class something to learn, often by heart; this might be a new grammar point, one or more irregular verbs, or a vocabulary list. Teachers check that this type of homework has been done by questioning both individuals and/or the entire class, as well as setting short tests for which marks and grades will sometimes be recorded.

It is important to regard each type of homework as being of equal importance. Many students make the mistake of taking informal and learning homework less seriously than formal homework. What you have to bear in mind is that the above types of homework are part of your teacher's overall strategy to ensure that you learn your language as effectively as possible.

It may be that at times you cannot see the point of a particular homework assignment and so you neglect to do it (in my experience, this happens most often with learning homework). This is a dangerous path to follow, as undone homework has a nasty habit of catching up with you. Not only will you irritate your teacher, but you will also miss out on valuable parts of the coursework. Think of it this way—doing foreign language homework is like making up a patchwork quilt. If you miss out some of the patches, then the quilt will be next to useless. Undone homework has the effect of leaving large gaps in your overall knowledge and skill levels; just like the gaps in the patchwork quilt, they can seriously affect your progress.

Decide early on that you are going to put maximum effort into each piece of homework, and take responsibility for ensuring that this happens. What I'll now show you are the most effective ways in which you can manage your own homework commitments.

Doing Homework Effectively

Let's start off with the basics. What I would now like you to do is to read the advice I give on forward planning, time management and presentation of work (pages 28–31). These are all very relevant to the doing of homework, and you should take especial note of them. I would also like to add the following points:

- **Find somewhere suitable.** It is very important that you find the right place in which to do your foreign language homework. You may be lucky and have somewhere at home where you can get on with the task in hand without being disturbed or distracted; if not, then try going to your local library or investigate the possibility of staying on at your place of learning and doing your homework there (many institutions offer homework clubs where students can get peace and quiet in which to work, as well as being able to ask teachers for help and advice).

Wherever you do your homework, try to ensure that you have plenty of light and space, as well as a comfortable seat. Good posture is also important; sit at a table or desk rather than sprawl in an armchair. Try to find somewhere reasonably quiet, unless you are one of those lucky people who can work effectively in a noisy environment or with music playing in the background.

Finally, make sure that you take regular breaks. Work in concentrated spells until you begin to feel tired, then leave your homework for a while and go away and do something completely different. You'll find that when you return to your homework your mind and body will be refreshed, and you'll make better and quicker progress.

This technique is especially suited to two different types of foreign language homework: learning vocabulary and writing essays. In the first instance, trying to commit something to memory is quite an intensive and laborious process, and if you try to cram your brain with too much vocabulary in too short a time, you will find that you will be unable to retain it long term. Better to take things in small chunks; do a bit, walk away from it, and then come back later to continue the process.

As for essay writing, you will find that when you are working away intensely at a piece for a long period of time your brain will inevitably become tired, and you will start to make more mistakes than usual. The problem here is that you are so involved in the work you are doing that you cannot spot the errors you have made. If you take a break and come back to your essay, you will see these same errors immediately and correct them. It's all a question of avoiding what I call *brain overload* and making sure that your grey matter is regularly rested.

Remember that foreign language homework is, by its very nature, much more intensive than the norm. This is because you will often be working in the foreign language, a language with which you may not be entirely familiar or confident. To do this well you therefore require additional concentration, but to keep the concentration up you need a suitable place in which to work and regular breaks. That way, you'll achieve much better results and avoid the stress that homework often brings about.

- **Correct and redraft.** It's no use doing homework if you don't learn from it. Earlier in this chapter I stated that one of the reasons for giving homework was to provide students with a good idea of their strengths and weaknesses, as well as show them what they have to do to improve. This will only work if students take time to review their corrected homework. I therefore recommend that you take the following steps with every piece of homework that you receive back from your teacher:

  - Read it over carefully, noting the comments or corrections your teacher has made.

- Make sure that you understand why you made any mistakes. If you don't, ask your teacher for an explanation.

- If you have written something incorrectly in the foreign language, then rewrite it properly in what I call an *error log*. This is simply a list of corrected errors that you keep separately from your homework; if you regularly update it, you will have a continuous record of the most common errors you have been making. The fact that you are rewriting each corrected error also lessens the chance of making the same error in future.

- With longer pieces of imaginative writing (e.g. essays) you may wish to consider a full or partial rewrite (see the advice I gave on redrafting on pages 80–83). Give this to your teacher for remarking.

- Keep a record of homework attainment. This is a sheet of paper on which you record the following details for every piece of corrected homework you receive: the date it was done, a description of the homework task, the grade or mark you received, and any comments made by the teacher. If you do this regularly you will have a complete record of all the homework you have done for the class. You can also see at a glance how you have been doing, and which areas of your language learning need more attention. It is also a good idea to include details of any redrafted pieces of work you may have completed; that way you can compare your new grade, mark and/or teacher comment with the original. Homework attainment records can be highly-motivating for students, and are also useful summaries for parents to consult.

- Finally, make sure that you file your homework efficiently (see the advice I give on filing on pages 33–34). Homework pieces can be a valuable revision source, so make sure you retain them in an accessible location.

- **Go beyond the homework.** Let's think for a moment about the word *homework*. The first thing that springs to mind are exercises that your teacher has asked to be completed at home; in other words, precisely-defined tasks to be done within a strict time-scale outside your place of learning. Not a bad definition of homework, you might think. However, let me offer an alternative interpretation: homework is not only the work that you are *told* to do at home, but also the work that you *choose* to do at home. What I am trying to say here is that you should always try to go *beyond* the homework you have been set by doing something extra on your own initiative. Research has shown that the most effective language learners are those who take responsibility for their own learning. Do this by repeatedly asking yourself this question: *Now that I've* *completed the official homework, which aspect of my language learning can I devote some extra time to?* Here are some ideas for you to consider:

- **Ask for more.** Imagine that you are Oliver Twist and get into the habit of asking for more: not food, but homework. Unlike Oliver you'll get a positive response from teachers, who will be delighted to give you additional exercises to do (after all, it's a request that they don't often hear!). This is probably a better idea than making your own choice of extra work; the danger with this approach is that you stray onto areas that you don't yet fully understand, or that the teacher has reserved for future lessons or homework tasks. However, you may be confident enough to work in this way—it all depends on your ability as a language learner and the nature of the course you are following.

- **Read over the day's work.** Get into the habit of reading over the work you have done that day in class—that way you can revise material while it is still fresh in your mind.

- **Review your vocabulary.** Your textbook may have lists of vocabulary arranged by topic, or you may have been noting down miscellaneous vocabulary in your exercise book or notebook. Try to spend some time looking this over—it's surprising how much you can learn if you do this regularly, and you'll find that the process is relatively painless.

- **Practise your key skills.** In Part Two of this book (*Practice Makes Perfect*) I talk about many of the ways in which you can actively practise the four key skills of listening, speaking, reading and writing. Each of the four chapters in this part of the book have a section entitled *Work On Your…Skills*; what I recommend that you do is read over these sections and act on the advice that they contain.

The Final Word

At the end of the day, doing homework properly takes time. It cannot be rushed, and should never be neglected. To succeed in learning a foreign language you have to accept that much of your learning will take place outside the classroom, and give it the importance it deserves.

One other thing: homework is one of the vital links that exist between teacher and student. It is your chance to excel, to show your teacher what you know, to impress him or her with your hard work and diligence. If you remove that link by neglecting your homework, then what you are doing is severing one of the most important lines of communication in the teacher-student relationship. Like all relationships, this one has to be nurtured, and the best way of doing that is to ensure that you keep in regular touch with your teacher by completing all your homework assignments.

If you don't, then you make it difficult (if not impossible) for your teacher to assess your performance and suggest ways in which you can improve. So the next time you get a piece of homework, look on it as a learning opportunity and not as a necessary evil. All play and no homework makes Jack (and Jill) very dull linguists indeed.

Sitting Examinations

The mere mention of the word *examination* can have a variety of different effects on foreign language students. These range from instant feelings of fear, dread and panic all the way through to calm reflection on what lies ahead. Most of us are somewhere in the middle: a little nervous or concerned about how well we are likely to do.

It is true to say that the format of foreign language examinations is somewhat different from that of other subjects. For a start, you may be required to do practical examinations (such as orals or listening tests) where your performance depends to a great extent on how well you can cope with the unexpected and having to think on your feet. Even something as seemingly straightforward as a reading skills examination can make considerable demands on your vocabulary recall and your ability to deal with large chunks of text in a foreign (and not entirely familiar) language. Examinations that assess your skill in writing in the foreign language can also severely test your time management skills: not only have you to plan what you are going to write, but you also have to check it over thoroughly once it is written.

Finally, there is the question of the syllabus. Other subjects usually present you with a list of precise, manageable areas of knowledge that you are required to master, with the understanding that the final examination will be based exclusively on these same areas. Unfortunately, this doesn't always happen in foreign languages. Ask a foreign languages teacher what the syllabus is and you may get this answer: *all human life*. This means that students sitting a foreign languages examination have to cope with the unexpected, as a whole range of different topics may well present themselves.

Performing well is therefore not a question of mastering a limited body of knowledge and regurgitating it at the appropriate moment; it is more a test of how well you can apply the *skills* you have learnt to the task in question. Having said this, you also need to master the technique of preparing for and sitting examinations. The remainder of this chapter will give you some useful advice on how to do exactly that.

Know the Facts

The road to good examination performance in foreign languages starts with doing a bit of individual research. This involves finding out the following pieces of information about the examination(s) you will eventually be sitting:

- **The type of examination.** Make sure that you know the precise nature of the examination. Foreign language examinations often concentrate on one or more of the four key skills: listening, speaking, reading and writing. Here are a few examples: a speaking examination obviously tests your speaking skills but also requires you to listen to what the other person is saying. A listening paper may assess your ability to listen to and to understand what someone is saying, only then to ask you to write out in the foreign language your own views on the subject. So start off by finding out exactly which skill(s) will be required; once you know this you will be able to plan your revision accordingly.

- **What you should study.** Having identified the skill(s) to be tested, you should now give some thought to how best you can practise. (I would suggest once again that you re-read Part Two of this book (*Practice Makes Perfect*), as each of the four chapters has a section entitled *Work On Your...Skills* where effective methods of practice are fully described.) The other thing to consider is which topic areas, points of grammar, vocabulary sections, etc. are relevant to the examination you are sitting; consult your teacher should you require guidance here. Once you know what you have to study and the skills that go with it, you will be ready to make up your revision plan—a process I shall describe in the next section.

- **The examination format.** The examination may be split into more than one paper, with individual papers often divided into different sections. Acquaint yourself with the examination format by either consulting your teacher or having a look at previous examinations. Another thing to consider is timings: how long does each paper last, and how long should you spend on individual sections? Careful planning is required here, as time will be at a premium when the examination begins.

- **The level at which you are sitting.** Certain examinations are offered at different levels of difficulty, with teachers entering their students for the level most suited to their progress and ability. Make sure that you know the level at which you have been entered.

- **The date, time and venue.** This may seem obvious, but it is vital that you take careful note of these details. It's no use studying hard for an examination that you miss through your own carelessness!

Revising for Examinations

It's now time to consider how exactly you are going to manage your revision. If you have done all the things covered in the last section, then you will know precisely what lies ahead of you and what you have to revise or practise. This is a dangerous point for many students; despite being well acquainted with the examination and its requirements, many are unable to devise an effective plan of study. The result is that they sit the examination without having done any continuous and thorough revision, and fail to achieve the desired result. This scenario can easily be avoided if you follow this advice:

- **Give yourself enough time to revise.** It's no use waiting until the night before the examination and then desperately trying to cram in as much material as you can—it just won't work. Your brain will suffer from information overload and refuse to digest what you are feeding it. When you realise that this is happening you will become even more anxious and panic-stricken, with the result that you will probably sleep badly and go into the examination feeling both physically and nervously exhausted. It is therefore essential that you make a conscious decision to start revising well before the examination takes place. How long before, you may ask. Unfortunately there is no clear answer to this; it all depends on the nature of the examination and your own state of readiness. If in doubt, ask your teacher for advice.

- **Make up a revision plan.** Once you have decided when to start revising, sit down and work out a revision plan for your foreign language examinations. This is quite simply a list of times at which you intend revising; as such, it may be part of a larger plan involving other subjects for which you will have to sit examinations. (The format of the plan is up to you, but I recommend that you read the *Forward Planning* and *Time Management* sections on pages 28–30; these contain useful general advice that is also relevant to the construction of an effective revision plan.) One other tip: try to revise in short spells, giving yourself regular breaks. That way your brain will get a chance to breathe!

- **Choose your revision activities.** Part of the problem in making up a revision plan is knowing exactly what it is that you are supposed to be revising and how best you can do this. Obviously it all depends on the nature and format of the examination that you are going to be sitting, and you may wish to take specialist advice from your teacher. However, you may find it useful to read through the following key revision activities, bearing in mind that not all of them will be relevant to your own particular needs and circumstances:

- **Work through some past papers.** If you are sitting a public examination, try to ensure that you work through some of the papers set in previous years. By doing this you will become familiar with the format of the examination, as well as the level, style and content of the various items. Knowing exactly what to expect when you enter the examination hall makes you feel less nervous, and so gives you that little bit of extra confidence.

  It may be that your teacher will have already worked through some of the past papers with you or set them as homework assignments; if this is the case, try to get extra practice by doing those that your teacher has not had time to tackle. Many of the major examining boards now issue booklets of past papers that can be purchased by students. These are convenient to use, but you may find that they are only issued for the more popular foreign languages, and often cover a limited number of years. An alternative solution is to ask your teacher to lend you some; this way you can be sure of getting exactly what you require, as most foreign languages departments maintain their own archives of past papers.

  Finally, you may be able to access past papers through your place of learning or local library, or possibly on-line. One other thing: when you work through past papers as part of your revision plan, try to do some of them under test conditions. This enables you to get a feel for the paper and the time required to complete it; the experience may also reveal language matters that you might want to brush up on or revise in greater depth.

- **Revise your vocabulary.** It makes sense to put a lot of time and effort into revising your vocabulary. After all, words are the building bricks of language and without them you can do nothing. Many students neglect the learning of vocabulary, especially when the use of a dictionary is permitted during the examination. This approach is a dangerous one; looking up words that you ought to know (but don't) wastes a lot of valuable time. Furthermore, dictionaries cannot really help you during speaking or listening examinations. The most successful students are therefore those who possess the widest vocabulary base and can recall it from memory. To get to this point requires a good deal of time and effort, and there are not really any shortcuts.

The first thing you should do, therefore, is to identify well before the examination the body of vocabulary that you intend to revise. For example, your coursebook may have vocabulary sections arranged by topic area, or you may have a separate vocabulary book; it may be that your teacher has issued you with vocabulary sheets, or you may have been keeping your own vocabulary file (see page 62); alternatively, your sources of vocabulary may be a mixture of the above. Once you have decided what vocabulary you are to revise, split it into manageable chunks that can be done on a daily basis, and therefore retained more easily in your memory.

What, you may ask, is the best way of revising vocabulary? One approach that I recommend to students is called *Look, Cover, Write and Check*. This is how it works: take each word individually, and *look* at it while trying to form a picture of the spelling in your head, along with its English meaning. (Very occasionally you may be able to associate the sound or spelling of the word with an English word that has some connection or resemblance to it. A couple of examples will show you what I mean. In Italian the word *capelli* means hair; one way of remembering the meaning would be to imagine a *cap* covering your hair. Similarly, in French the verb *dormir* means to sleep; just think of a *dormitory* and you'll remember the meaning.)

Once you have *looked* at the word, the next step is to *cover* it up, then try to *write* both the word and its meaning from memory. After doing this, you then *check* that you have the correct spelling and meaning. If you don't, then go back to the beginning and try again. This can sound a tedious process, but it does work.

Why not make it a little more interesting by involving someone else? That way, you can skip the *look* and *cover* phases and just ask the other person to ask you words at random, which you then *write* and *check*. Or you can just give the answers and check them orally, if you prefer. Whatever system you go for, remember that you have to revise regularly and methodically in order to achieve maximum results.

- **Go over your grammar and verbs.** This is the bit that many students hate! In the previous section I said that words were *the building bricks of language*, but unless you have a plan for fitting the bricks together then you won't be able to build anything. Grammar provides that plan by setting out precise rules to be followed when we combine words to form sentences. Anyone who therefore tries to learn a language without learning its grammar is doomed to failure, as he or she will never progress beyond the stage of one-word utterances and pre-learned phrases. Any revision plan you make up must therefore pay adequate attention to those grammar points covered during your course. These will be listed either in your grammar file (if you have kept one; see page 62) or in your textbook (see page 90). Read over your notes for each grammar point, and then try to follow these up by doing some exercises (ask your teacher if you are unable to locate any).

Finally, be sure to revise your *verbs*. Start by making sure that you know how to form any tenses you have been taught, what their meaning is and in which contexts they should be used. Remember that all foreign languages have certain verbs that are *irregular*, that is to say they do not follow the usual rules. Look these over and ensure that you are familiar with the most common of them; your teacher can give you valuable advice here, as well as suggesting extra exercises you can do. Any time spent on brushing up on your verbs is time well spent; after all, a verb is a *doing* word, and without them we can *do* nothing.

- **Read over your work.** Examinations usually come at the end of a term or year's work. During that time you will have been consistently working away, both at your place of learning as well as at home. You will probably have filled exercise books, notebooks and countless sheets of paper with exercises, essays and class tests, all set by your teacher to enable you to prac- tise and assess what you have learnt.

Now is the time to reconsider this mass of work by reading it through and incorporating it into your revision plan. (This is a lot easier if you have been filing and storing your work carefully; see pages 32–34.) What do I mean by this? For example, if you have written any essays in the foreign language then read them over again and take care to do the following: consider the mistakes you made and how you intend to avoid them in future, make a note of vocabulary and phrases that you used successfully, and rewrite sec- tions you are not entirely happy with (see pages 80–83).

Alternatively, reading over any grammar exercises you may have already done is often a good way of revising the grammar point itself. Or how about this: read over any class tests you have done, as they may remind you of areas you might have forgotten to revise. Remember that what you have done in the past is the key to what you will do in the future, so think of your past work as a resource that you can dip into while preparing for what lies ahead.

Finally, let me remind you of a quick solution to the question of which revision activities you opt for. If you are learning one of the more popular foreign languages and are about to sit a public examination in it, the chances are that publishers will have issued a study guide for your language and level. These guides include many useful features such as information on examination format, the syllabus, vocabulary/grammar sections and practice materials. Many students find these convenient to use, and they are well worth considering. Remember, however, that buying a guide will not automatically make you pass—it's how you use it that counts, and at the end of the day the only sure way of passing examinations is to work as hard as possible.

- **Find somewhere suitable to revise.** Effective revision requires a place where you can work efficiently. (Normally this will be the same location at which you do homework; see page 107.) Obviously the place you choose to revise may depend on the nature of the work you require to do. For example, a public library is obviously not an ideal place to record yourself speaking the foreign language; similarly, if you are practising an oral with a friend, pick a place where you can talk away without others listening in or interrupting you.

Sitting Examinations

You've done all the studying, and you're now about to sit the examination. How are you feeling? The answer will depend on largely on the kind of person you are, and how you cope with a potentially stressful situation. Some of us brim with self-confidence and assurance when we enter the examination hall, whereas others become nervous wrecks. There are dangers for both types of people: if you are over-confident, you risk underestimating the difficulties posed by the examination, whereas nervousness can prevent you from settling down and doing your best. It is important to try to steer a middle course: you should be reasonably relaxed and confident, but slightly nervous and apprehensive. Getting into this frame of mind becomes very much easier if you follow this common sense advice:

Before the Examination

- **Take it easy the night before.** Try to avoid studying too intensively the night before the examination—at this late stage it probably won't do you much good. It's a much better idea to have a quick, last look at your revision notes and then relax for the rest of the evening. That way, when you go to bed your mind will be sufficiently distracted to allow you to have a good night's sleep. Try to avoid going to bed too early—sometimes this can be counterproductive as you are not tired enough to fall asleep quickly, with the result that you lie awake thinking anxiously about the examination.

- **Don't skip breakfast.** Both body and brain need nourishment for the task ahead of you, so get off to a good start by having a reasonable breakfast. This will ensure that your blood sugar level will not drop off during the examination.

- **Turn up for the examination in good time.** There is nothing worse than turning up for an examination late. You get yourself off to the worst possible start and disrupt others. You also run the risk of not being admitted to the examination hall, especially if you are sitting a test in listening. So be there early! (Having said this, it is not a good idea to arrive too early, as waiting for too long a time can increase your nervousness. This is especially true for oral examinations, where you are normally expected to start speaking as soon as you enter the examination room: there is no time, therefore, to sit down and quietly compose yourself as you would do before a written examination.)

During the Examination

- **Read all about it.** Read the instructions on the question paper carefully—sometimes these are given in the foreign language and can be easily misunderstood.

- **Think before you write.** It can be quite tempting to rush to get something down on paper, but time spent in thoughtful reflection makes for clearer and more effective responses.

- **Presentation is important.** Present your answers neatly, clearly and legibly. You may wish to consider using double-spacing (i.e. write on a line, then miss a line), so that mistakes can be quickly scored out and corrections inserted into the line above—this is much better than using correcting fluid and having to wait until it dries.

- **Give concise answers.** When doing listening and reading comprehension exercises, it often preferable to give your answers in note form rather than complete sentences, as long as you include the correct amount of detail.

- **Use your dictionary effectively.** Dictionaries can be a great help, but you can waste a lot of time by using them ineffectively. See pages 99–104 for clear advice on how to avoid this.

- **Leave enough time for checking.** Time management during examinations is crucially important. Bring along an accurate watch and check the time allocation for the paper before you start. Make sure that you leave enough time to read over your answers; this is especially important if you have been writing in the foreign language, as it is much easier to make mistakes here (see pages 74–77 for help on checking work).

- **Keep your cool.** It's all too easy to panic during foreign language examinations, especially when they involve listening and speaking. Try to stay calm by slowing yourself down, taking a deep breath and saying to yourself that you are going to deal with this problem, whatever it might be. You have to be both positive and firm with yourself in order to do this, otherwise the nerves will take over. Grit your teeth and keep yourself focused on the task in hand; if you do this, you will overcome the difficulty and regain your confidence. It might help you to remember an old saying: *When the going gets tough, the tough get going.*

After the Examination

- **Don't compare notes with your friends.** When you come out of the examination hall, the great temptation is to approach your friends and ask them how they got on. Before you know it you will be comparing answers you gave, which is fine if they happen to be the correct ones—but what if they are not? You go home regretting you didn't say or write a particular thing. You begin to run through the entire examination in your mind, trying to recall your responses. You get depressed because you realise that you may have given the wrong answers. Teachers have a name for this process of after-exam analysis; they call it a *post mortem*. My advice to you is not to carry them out. Think of it this way; what is done is done, and no amount of agonising is going to change the result. So why worry about it?

- **What if I fail?** It's not the end of the world. You will probably be able to re-sit at a later stage. If it is an examination held by your place of learning, you will undoubtedly get some feedback about where you went wrong, and the chance to go over the paper with your teacher. Make the most of this opportunity, and consider your temporary failure as a stepping-stone towards your eventual success. Think positive, and you will achieve a positive result.

The Final Word

Examinations are an imperfect way of assessing knowledge, especially when you are studying a foreign language. You may sit an oral examination and think to yourself, *I could have said that but I didn't*. You might ponder over the examination essay you have just written and regret that it wasn't on your favourite subject. The examination reading comprehension that you found particularly difficult may have dealt with a topic whose vocabulary was unfamiliar to you. Then there was the listening examination—just a little too fast for comfort, and not enough time to write down the answers.

Yes, examinations (and not only those in foreign languages) can be unfair, as they do not always test what we know; indeed, some would say that they do the exact opposite. The truth, however, is that examinations (despite all their perceived faults and limitations) are society's preferred system of assessing our knowledge and ability. If we want to get anywhere in our study of a foreign language, then we have to accept that they are a fundamental part of the process and have to be passed. I hope that by acting on the advice given in this chapter you will be able to do exactly that.

PART IV

Living the Language

Using Computers

People often ask me if computers can help them to learn a foreign language. I tell them yes, as long as they are aware of these facts:

- You don't have to use a computer to become a good linguist. They can make many aspects of language learning easier, quicker and more enjoyable, but you *can* do without them.

- You should feel comfortable and confident about using them. If you don't but still want to have a go, then brush up on your basic computer skills before proceeding—this will save you time in the long run.

- Computers can only *help* you to learn a foreign language; they cannot work miracles. The technology sometimes makes us forget this; we expect wonderful things to happen at the push of a button, but it's never quite as simple as that!

You might now be thinking that I don't really like computers, but you would be totally wrong. I love them, and have spent a considerable part of my life working with them. I suppose I'm being just a little bit cautious here, as I don't want to give the impression that using computers in foreign language studies is something that we should *all* be doing. Variety is the spice of life when learning a foreign language, and the computer is only one of a wide range of effective techniques and resources. Having said that, it can prove to be a valuable one, and we should certainly not ignore it. If you do decide that you want to use computers, then welcome aboard—this chapter will help you to get the most out of them. Let's start off by listing the major ways in which computers can help you to learn a foreign language:

- Word processors allow you to present and store your written work.

- There is a good range of software available that can help you improve in all four key skills and teach you new vocabulary.

- The Internet provides a large number of sites of great interest to foreign language learners.

- Computers offer a quick and easy way of establishing and maintaining contact with both teachers, fellow students and speakers of the foreign language you are learning.

Let's now look at each of these areas in greater detail.

Word Processing

Being able to word-process a piece of writing presents a number of advantages to the language learner:

- **Appearance.** No matter how good your handwriting is, your written work will always look better if it is word-processed. This is because you have complete control over all aspects of the document: size of margins, choice and size of fonts, line spacing and justification, insertion of clip art, etc. The possibilities are endless, and that is where the dangers begin. Many students become fascinated with all the various options available and tend to spend too much time on appearance. They use a variety of fonts and other decorative effects (e.g. different text colours, elaborate borders and a wealth of clip art), ending up with a document that is actually more difficult to read. The time spent on presentation is often at the expense of content, so while the illustrations might be very fetching the text will be riddled with mistakes.

  The way to avoid this is to keep things simple. Stick to one clear, common font and don't make it too small (my own particular favourites are Arial, Times New Roman and Verdana, all in fourteen point). Don't overdo decorative effects such as clip art; remember that *less* is *more*. Try to use double line spacing; that way the teacher can easily insert comments. Finally, when you print out make sure that the print quality is sufficiently high, as draft mode can look a little indistinct. The overall result will be a document that is a pleasure to read and may give you a better chance of achieving a good grade.

- **Editing.** Word processors make it extremely easy to add, delete and modify our work. This is a positive advantage when writing creatively in the foreign language, as the process of amending and rewriting your work (see pages 80–83) becomes much quicker. One key feature of many word processors is their ability to *spellcheck* a document. This can be a powerful tool, provided that you have access to a spellchecker in the foreign language. These are available for many of the popular word processing programs, but are often quite expensive. Your place of learning may have one already installed on one of their own machines that you might be permitted to use; why not ask? One other advantage of many spellcheckers is that they can often give advice about grammar and sentence construction.

However, if you have to proof-read your document the old-fashioned way (see pages 74–77), then I recommend that you do this from a print-out rather than from the screen. The reason for this is that it is more difficult and tiring for the eye to spot mistakes displayed on a screen, as you cannot easily cover the text you are not checking.

- **Storage.** Being able to word-process your work means that you can save your documents quickly and easily and retrieve them at a later date. There is the added advantage of being able to create various folders on your computer in which you can store different areas of your work. For example, you might have different folders for grammar, vocabulary, essays, homework, etc. However, a few words of caution. When word processing your work, get into the habit of saving the document at regular intervals (e.g. every five minutes). If you do this then you avoid losing your work should the computer suddenly decide to crash. (Many word processing programs will save your document automatically for you, but I always like to make sure by doing it myself.)

  It is good practice whenever you're saving your final version of a document to take the time to save a second copy to a different location. So if you save your latest essay directly to your computer's hard drive, make sure that you save a copy to a floppy disk (or any other form of removable storage) and store it away from the computer. That way, if your computer suffers a hard disk failure you will not lose everything that you have stored on it, as you will have back-up copies that you can use to reload your files.

  Try to keep a paper copy of everything that you store on your computer; this can be used both for reference purposes as well as a safeguard against both your hard drive failing *and* your removable storage being mislaid or developing a fault, as you can then arrange to have your paper copies scanned in to your computer using word recognition software (this can be complicated and should only be done as a last resort; ask for advice on how you should go about doing this).

- **Distribution.** Computers allow you to send your work easily to others. For example, you may wish to share your grammar notes with a fellow student or hand in homework to your teacher. This can be done either by saving your document to a floppy disk and handing in directly to the other person, or by sending it as an attachment to an e-mail.

Finally, a few points to consider about word processing. The first regards your typing skills—are they up to scratch? I'm asking you this because it is a bad idea to word-process your work if poor typing leads you to make more mistakes than if you had written it by hand. Better an accurate, hand-written piece of work than a word-processed collection of spelling errors.

Then there are accents. The language you are studying may require special accents to be entered above letters or particular characters to be used. If this is the case, find out the easiest way of doing this on your word processor. Usually you can insert accents and special characters by using one of the drop-down menus, or alternatively it may be possible to enter them directly from the keyboard. Whatever the solution, find out what it is and practise entering them until you are fluent. This is much better than simply adding them in by hand afterwards, as it gives your document a much more professional look and feel.

Language Learning Software

There is a wide range of software available that can help you with many different areas of your language learning, such as vocabulary, grammar, pronunciation, listening skills, etc. Many of these programs offer combinations of these areas presented in the form of topics (see pages 89–90), although there are some that concentrate on one feature or function only (e.g. translation software).

Most language learning software is easily available commercially from retail outlets or the Internet, but choosing the right program can be a tricky process. The problem is that we tend to rely on our instincts rather than consider things logically. We read the back cover of the package, look at a few illustrations of what the software looks like in action, try to imagine how good it might be, and finally buy it on the off-chance that it's what we are looking for. The result is often disappointment; once the program is installed on your computer and you have had time to evaluate it properly, you often find that is doesn't live up to expectations. How can this be avoided? One solution is to ask yourself these questions before making any software purchase:

- **What am I looking for?** Try to get clear in your mind what your needs are. Start off by identifying two things: the particular skills and/or topic areas that you wish to practise, and the level at which you are capable of working. Then do some research on the features of the program that you're considering. As I've already hinted, reading the description on the back of the box is not always the best way of doing this; you'll often find much more detailed information on the software publisher's website. You can then compare your own personal requirements with the features offered by the program, and form an initial impression of its suitability.

- **How good is this program?** A program may seem to include all the functions and features you require, but the crucial factor is how well it performs. The best way of finding out is to try the program before you buy it. This is not always possible at the point of sale, as most retailers lack the facilities to demonstrate individual programs to customers. If this is the case, try to find someone who has used the program and can give you advice, such as your teacher or fellow students.

Alternatively, the Internet can be a great source of information on these matters. Start off with the software publisher's website; sometimes a demo version will be available for you to try out on-line. Other websites may contain reviews of the program, either written by professionals or by people who have already bought it and want to tell you about their experiences. The best way of finding these reviews is to enter the name of the program into one of the popular search engines (e.g. *Google* or *Altavista*) and then investigate some of the links that appear.

- **Will it work on my computer?** Most language-learning programs have reasonably modest requirements and do not require the latest technology to get them up and running. However, as with all software make sure that you check that your system is compatible. The key areas to look at are as follows: operating system, processor speed, amount of memory required, video and sound card specifications, and CD-ROM speed. Some programs (such as translators and vocabulary builders) copy large files to memory, so you should ensure that you have enough space available on your hard disk.

The other key feature of many programs is audio: playing native speaker sound files, recording yourself speaking the foreign language and comparing it to the real thing, etc. Make sure that your audio components are up to the task: you will need a functioning soundcard, a pair of speakers and/or a set of headphones, and a microphone. Recording and playback is much easier if you invest in a headset (a set of headphones with a microphone attached) as you don't have to worry about holding or placing the microphone correctly.

Using the Internet

The Internet is perhaps the most valuable computer-based resource in foreign language learning and teaching. Those of you who have surfed the web need no reminder of the vast number of sites available, dealing with every subject imaginable. All human knowledge appears to be there, and that is the fundamental problem—how do we find what we are looking for amongst the hundreds of thousands of pages available? Before the Internet appeared, we used to say that *a little knowledge is a dangerous thing*; now the opposite seems to be true. Nevertheless, effective use of the web can pay enormous dividends for foreign language learners, provided that we are aware of the various possibilities available to us. Here are some of them, together with a short description and advice on how best they can be used:

- **Search engines.** If you don't have the exact address of a website (or are looking for a variety of sites on a particular subject) then the tool to use is a search engine. There are two main types: the first and most common (such as *Google* and *Altavista*) allows you to enter any number of words in a search box; one click of the mouse will then list all the sites in which those words appear, and then it's up to you to investigate whichever seem most relevant to your needs. It doesn't matter which language you use; as long as the spelling is correct, the search engine will track down the sites containing your word, and all is not lost if you misspell a word—what will happen is that the correct word will be suggested together with the helpful question, *Did you mean this?*

  This type of search engine is also very useful when you are translating from one language to another. This is how it works: let's suppose that you are translating from English into French and that you are unsure about a particular phrase you have written. No problem: enter it into the search engine within inverted commas, and the search engine will then look for occurrences of the *entire* phrase and not its individual words. That way, if the phrase is correct, you will be presented with examples of texts in which it occurs. If it isn't, the likelihood is that you won't find anything. (A word of caution; this only works with short phrases and not with long involved sentences, as the chances of somebody in the world writing a long sentence completely identical to your own are slim.)

  The second type of search engine is one that is particularly useful if you are looking for sites on a particular theme or topic. These allow to you browse individual subject categories and suggest relevant sites that you might visit. The best example of this type of search engine is *Yahoo!* (*www.yahoo.com*). If you take a look at its home page you'll see a series of links covering all the main areas of human knowledge and experience; click on any of these and you'll be presented with another list of links that cover further aspects of the subject in question. These are in turn subdivided, so that eventually you will reach a selection of sites relevant to your needs (this is known as a *hierarchical* search system).

The great thing about *Yahoo!* (and other search engines like it) is that they exist in different versions in different languages. These are normally listed as links on the home page, so that you can see at a glance which languages are available and reach them with a click of the mouse. Let's say, for example, that you are writing a French essay on healthy living and want to access some French web sites on the subject. No problem; just go to the French version of *Yahoo!* and follow the links until you arrive at what you are looking for.

- **On-line materials.** Language learners are especially well-served by the Internet, as there are numerous sites catering for every possible need (having said this, the more popular languages obviously have the widest coverage). These sites are run by a wide variety of providers: commercial publishers, language schools, broadcasters, primary and secondary schools, colleges and universities, local education authorities and individual teachers. Many of the resources on offer are free of charge to the user, and cover the full range of language activities. Here are some examples: grammar explanations and exercises, vocabulary lists, reading and listening exercises, video clips, background knowledge, games, quizzes, and even entire language courses. Some of these sites will often allow you to download materials and language learning programs.

How do you find all of this? Your first port of call should be a search engine; just key in what you're looking for (e.g. French perfect tense verb practice) and you'll be presented with a list of possible sites. Alternatively, check with your teacher; there may be specific websites that have already been identified by your place of learning (e.g. many commercial coursebooks now have their own website). Fellow students can also be a good source of useful sites; why not swap notes amongst yourselves?

- **On-line dictionaries.** The web offers a wide variety of on-line dictionaries in many different combinations of languages. All you do is type in the word you wish to translate and the answer arrives in a matter of seconds. These sites can be handy if you do not have access to a conventional dictionary, but in my experience many of them lack sufficient detail to be truly useful. What I mean by this is that they tend to offer a limited range of translations and examples when compared to the average paper dictionary. There is also the time factor to consider; is it really that much quicker than looking up the word in the traditional way?

- **On-line translators.** There are some sites that claim to be able to translate passages from one language to another. You are prompted to enter your text (there is usually a limit of about 150 words), after which you select the language into which the text is to be translated. Another click of the mouse and your translation appears—but beware, appearances can be deceptive! The translations produced by these sites are not fully accurate: they are what might be termed *approximate* translations. What does this mean? Sometimes the grammar will be wrong, other times the computer will have misinterpreted the proper meaning of a particular word. You do get a translation, but it is a rough and ready one. There are cases when this is all you require (e.g. when you only need to get the broad meaning of a text), but if accuracy is important then you have to take the time to revise the translation yourself.

  If you like the idea of using translation software then I recommend that you use one of the various commercial programs that are available. These offer a greater degree of accuracy than their website counterparts and have no word limit, but have two main disadvantages: they require a lot of memory to install and they tend to be expensive. What you should always remember is that translation is an art, and machines can never be quite as good as the human brain. I remember a story about a particular translation program that claimed to translate from English into Russian. This was being tested by a reviewer who typed in the English phrase *out of sight, out of mind*. What he got was the Russian for *invisible maniac*. You have been warned!

- **Personal communication.** It is true to say that computers have revolutionised the way in which people communicate with each other. Getting in touch with others is now easier, quicker and more convenient as more and more of us become computer literate. The main benefit for language learners is the possibility of two-way communication with speakers of the target language. This can be achieved by the following means: e-mail, voice messages, text chat and voice chat. Let's now have a closer look at each:

  - **E-mail.** There was a time when the only reasonably cheap way of communicating with someone abroad was by letter. As we all know, letters take time to arrive, and pen-friends are often late in replying—depending on whether or not they remember to stick on the correct stamps and pop it in the post-box! (This explains why some people refer to it as *snail mail*.) Now all we have to do is get on-line, type our message, send it, and before you know it your pen-friend has read it and replied. The whole process is so simple and straightforward that it encourages us to communicate, in much the same way as mobile phones and text messages keep us constantly in touch with each other.

The benefits for anyone learning a foreign language are immense—not only do you improve your writing skills, but you learn a lot about the other person, their background and the country in which they live. Sometimes friendships can develop that last for years, with pen-friends eventually meeting in person. But how do you go about finding an e-mail pen-friend? You could have a look at various sites on the Internet that offer to put you in touch with someone, but it's always a good idea to check out sites with your teacher before you sign up to anything. The best solution, to my mind, is to convince your teacher to organise a class e-mail link with an equivalent class in the foreign country. That way your teacher can devote some time during lessons to e-mail correspondence, and both classes can even arrange to exchange e-mails simultaneously. You also have the advantage of being able to ask your teacher for help and advice while writing.

How should you approach your e-mail correspondence? The first thing I recommend is that you write in both languages, and encourage your partner to do the same. It is probably a good idea to start off with each of you writing in your own native language; in this way you will get to know one another without some of the misunderstandings that can occur when writing in the foreign language, and you will both gain valuable reading comprehension practice.

During this phase you should concentrate on getting to know your partner. Don't be too curious or boastful, otherwise you may give offence. Once you both feel comfortable, each of you should try corresponding in the foreign language. At first it may prove to be difficult, but stick with it and gradually you will improve. Don't get too concerned about grammatical accuracy; your first priority is to communicate with your partner. As time goes on you will eventually help one another with areas of difficulty.

As I have said, the great thing about e-mail is that you can have a reply within seconds if both of you are on-line at the same time. But it isn't all about speed—those of us who prefer to take things a little slower can do exactly that. With e-mail, there is no pressure to perform instantly: you have time to think about, write and review your message before finally clicking *Send*.

One final thought: have you considered using e-mail as a means of communication between yourself and your teacher? This could involve such things as asking for help and sending homework via attachments. Many teachers are happy to operate in this way, and it is becoming easier to do so as more and more educational institutions develop their own computer networks.

- **Voice messages.** There comes a time in every exchange of e-mails when we would like to hear our correspondent's voice as well as read what they have to say to us. Of course, at this point you could quite simply reach for the telephone and give them a ring, but long-distance calls can often be expensive. Why not send them a voice message instead?

This is how you do it: most computers have a program already installed that allows you to record your voice, save it to disk and play it back (you'll obviously need a microphone to do this). Once you've recorded and saved your message, the next step is to attach the sound file to your next e-mail (get some help if you're unsure about how to do this). When your correspondent opens the e-mail, he or she will be able to download the attachment and play it back (provided the file is compatible—something you should also check out). A word of advice: don't make your message too long, as large sound files can use up a lot of memory and may take a long time to send as attachments.

- **Text chat.** This involves having a written conversation with someone while both of you are on-line. So you type in what you want to say, click the mouse and in a matter of seconds the other person's reply appears on your screen. You then continue the conversation for as long as you both wish.

The nature of text chat means that it is even more immediate than e-mail, with a much shorter time in which to consider and type your answer. There are various sites that offer text chat in a variety of languages, but I would advise you once again to get some advice as to their suitability. The main advantage of text chat as compared to e-mail is that you can talk to more than one person simultaneously. There is also the possibility of talking to a wider range of people, and being able to save to disk the conversations you have with them.

Finally, text chat (like e-mail) requires only an Internet connection to function. It's not for every language learner, as some people don't enjoy the element of unpredictability—not knowing which way a conversation might turn can place considerable demands on your language skills. However, if you are adventurous, enterprising and fairly confident linguistically, then text chat might be just the thing for you.

- **Voice chat.** Here the set-up is much the same as for text chat, with one big difference—you are now talking live on-line to other people. To do this you will need to be quite competent orally, as you will be conversing with native speakers. Don't be put off by this, as the people you will be talking to are obviously aware that you are learning their language and should adjust the pace and level accordingly. Remember that they are taking part because they want to have a conversation with you in English, so you have to show the same consideration.

One other thing: voice chat is also a great way of testing your listening skills, as you can't have a conversation without being able to understand what the other person is saying to you. If you're interested in voice chat then have a look at the same sites that offer e-mail partners and text chat, and remember the golden rule: treat everything you find on the Internet with the proper degree of care and caution. If you're unsure of a site, get someone to check it out for you.

Like its text equivalent, voice chat may only suit language learners who are confident orally and relish the prospect of talking live in the foreign language. Don't let this put you off having a try; after all, sometimes the best way of learning is to jump in at the deep end! One other thing: voice chat requires a headset with integrated microphone and a reliable Internet connection.

The Final Word

Few people will dispute the fact that computers can make learning a language more interesting and enjoyable. You may already be one of the many students who are computer enthusiasts and make full use of the excellent software available and the wide range of resources to be found on-line. Alternatively, you may be an occasional user who is considering investigating some of the possibilities I have described in this chapter. Or perhaps the thought of going near a computer fills you with fear and trepidation; if so, don't worry about it, you can still become an expert linguist!

At this point I would like to repeat what I said at the beginning of the chapter: whatever your situation, it is important to consider computers as just one of the many tools available to us when we learn a foreign language, and *not* to think that we cannot succeed without them. The problem is that we are often dazzled by the technology on display, and duped into believing that it is vital for our success. We have to take a step back and remind ourselves that computers cannot teach a foreign language at the touch of a button or the click of a mouse; you have to *work* if you want to succeed, and use all the energy, motivation, and brainpower at your disposal. As John F. Kennedy once remarked, *Man is still the most extraordinary computer of all.*

Sound and Vision

There was a time when the written word was the principal medium of education and communication. If we wished to acquire knowledge, then we had to do so through the printed page. Nations built vast libraries to store their ever-increasing archives of books and newspapers, and entire generations spent countless hours poring over them.

Nowadays, the written word is still important, but we are beginning to read it on our computer screens rather than from the pages of a book. We now look to other forms of electronic media to provide us with more instant knowledge and information, and this is delivered to us through *sound* and *vision*: television, video/DVD, radio and CD/cassette. The purpose of this chapter is to show how we can use these media to enhance our learning of a foreign language.

Television

Being able to view television programmes in the foreign language is now becoming much easier with the advent of satellite and cable systems, with many providers now offering packages that include a variety of foreign channels. With satellite systems much depends on where you are situated geographically, as a larger dish may be required to pick up certain stations; there may also be increased subscription charges. With cable networks you are limited to the channels your provider includes in your package.

If, for any reason, you are unable to access foreign language programmes at home through satellite or cable, then I suggest that you check if facilities exist in your place of learning. Many language departments have now invested in satellite or cable systems and actively encourage their students to view foreign language programmes as often as possible. If this is not the case, then the websites of major foreign television stations often include short video-clips of excerpts from their programmes; not as good as the real thing, but very much better than nothing.

If you are fortunate enough to be able to view live foreign language television, then what should you be watching? The following types of broadcasts are particularly useful for improving your language skills:

- **Advertisements.** These are effective because they are short, direct and to the point. The message you see is the same as the one you hear: buy this product! The fact that you can clearly see what is being advertised makes it much easier to understand what is being said about it. There is also the advantage of being able to view advertisements for products that you may already use or be familiar with; indeed, sometimes the advertisements themselves are identical to the ones you will have already viewed on your own country's television channels. So instead of switching over when the advertisements come on, sit and watch them all—you'll be surprised at what you might learn (and buy)!

- **Quiz shows.** Once you understand the format of a quiz show, it becomes much easier to follow the language being spoken in it. Many of the quiz shows we watch on television originate in Britain and the United States and are then syndicated all over the world, so there's a good chance that we'll be viewing a foreign version of a programme that we already know and enjoy.

- **Soaps and sitcoms.** Love them or hate them, soaps and sitcoms are an essential element of television programming. You may be lucky enough to come across foreign language versions of programmes you already view in your own language, in which case your familiarity with the characters and story-lines will help with comprehension. These kind of programmes are also seriously addictive, which is a great thing if you are learning a language—after all, you can never get enough practice!

- **News and current affairs.** These are especially valuable as the pictures always illustrate the news being reported. One effective strategy is to watch a news or current affairs programme first in your own language, so that you are perfectly informed about all that has happened in the world on that particular day; then, when you watch the equivalent programme in the foreign language, you will see the same items being reported and be able to understand them much better than if you were viewing them for the first time.

What about those of us who have no access to satellite or cable broadcasts in the foreign language? I've already mentioned using the Internet, but there are a couple of areas served by terrestrial stations. The first of these is foreign language broadcasts aimed at educational institutions. These cover a number of different languages and range from entire courses to individual programmes on specific topic areas and/or cultural issues. (In some cases they may be directly linked to the coursebook that you are using at your place of learning.) How do you find out what is being shown and when? You can always search the programme listings, but a much easier way is to ask your teacher—many television channels have education units that regularly send out details of programming to educational institutions. One drawback is that these programmes are sometimes shown at inconvenient times, so it helps if you have access to a video recorder.

The second area is foreign language films. Many terrestrial channels often show these with the original soundtrack but with English subtitles. Reading these as you watch the film can be an effective learning experience, as you get instant confirmation of what the characters are saying as well as the chance to compare the accuracy of the subtitles to the original dialogue. If you don't want to do this, then I suggest covering the bottom of the screen with a piece of card; that way, you can test how much you understand, with the advantage that you can remove the card if the going gets too tough!

The question of film subtitles and whether or not to use them brings us back to satellite and cable broadcasts. Many of the foreign language programmes that you view will have subtitles that you can access through teletext, so you have the option of reading as well as hearing what is being said. As we already know, this is an excellent way of consolidating your listening skills, and I recommend that you make full use of it. If you feel you can manage on your own, then all you have to do is switch off the subtitles—nothing could be simpler.

Video and DVD

One of the problems of watching live television is that we only get to view the programme once—unless we have a video recorder, in which case we can record it and play it back as many times as we wish. The benefits of being able to review and replay sections of a programme are obvious for language learners—if you don't understand what is being said the first time, then you have the possibility of playing it again and again until the message becomes clear. This process of repetition of language makes it easier for us to internalise what we are hearing, so if you are able to view foreign language programmes and record them, then you have a powerful learning tool that you should use to your advantage. (One word of caution: remember that most programmes are copyright.)

Another way of using video to support your language learning is to explore the wide range of commercial resources now available. These include entire language courses, reissues of language programmes already broadcast on television, foreign language films and documentaries, travel and cultural affairs programmes, etc. Buying these can often be quite expensive, but many local libraries now stock collections of foreign language videocassettes that you can either borrow free of charge or for a small fee. (Your place of learning library may also offer this service.) You should also look in video rental shops—often these will have a selection of foreign language items. If you decide that you want to buy, then there are many Internet sites that offer a wider range of foreign language videos than you might find in the shops.

I've already mentioned how watching foreign films can be a great way of learning a language. You may be able to view these live on television, or perhaps you will be lucky enough to find a cinema showing them (many do regular seasons of foreign language films, so check the press for details). However, the best way to watch these films is on video or DVD. I suggest to my students that they start off by choosing English language films that they have already seen and then view the foreign language version. The idea is that if you watch your favourite Hollywood blockbuster in the foreign language, then you will be able to follow the dialogue much more effectively as you already have a clear idea of what it is all about. (The only problem with this is that the original soundtrack will have been dubbed into the foreign language, so your favourite actor may have a totally different voice.) You may also find some films that retain the original English soundtrack but have foreign language subtitles. Alternatively, you may wish to look out for original foreign language films that may come with or without English subtitles.

At this point I'd like to say a word about DVD. This is now replacing VHS video, and offers several significant advantages to the language learner. We all know how difficult and time-consuming it can be to locate a particular section of tape on videocassette. DVD, on the other hand, resembles CD in the ease with which we can locate precise replay points. There are also none of the problems that occur with videocassettes, such as wear and tear, jamming, poor picture quality, etc. However, the most useful feature of DVD's is the ability to select both subtitles and soundtracks in a variety of different languages. Let me give you an example: you could watch your favourite feature film with the French soundtrack and English subtitles, or with the German soundtrack and Italian subtitles, or you could decide to view subtitles only without the soundtrack, or vice versa. (I should perhaps add that these options are only possible if they are already encoded on the particular DVD you are viewing.)

Radio

Many students tend to overlook radio as a foreign language source. This is a pity, because listening to the spoken word without any visual support forces us to concentrate totally on what we are hearing, a process that in time will considerably improve our listening skills. The easiest type of radio programmes to access are those broadcast by national stations within our own country. These consist mostly of educational transmissions aimed at foreign language learners, and are sometimes linked to television programmes and/or complete courses marketed by the television channel. Once again the best way to find out what is available (and whether or not it will be suitable) is to have a word with your teacher. You may also decide to record the programmes, although you should bear in mind the usual issues regarding copyright.

The alternative is to listen to live foreign stations. This can be rewarding, as you get the opportunity to listen to material aimed at native speakers. Reception is the main issue here; much depends on where you live, the quality of your radio and the location and transmitting power of the foreign stations. The best approach is to switch on your radio, extend the aerial (if you have one), turn the tuning dial and see what you can pick up. Avoid FM; the limited range of its transmitters means that it is unlikely that you will receive any foreign stations. Medium and short wave are much more productive, especially in the evening or at night when reception tends to be better. If you find an interesting station, you can either store it or make a note of the wavelength so that you can return to it in future. Alternatively, you can attempt to find particular stations by tuning in to the precise wavelength (there are a number of Internet sites that give this information).

You can also use the web to listen directly to a wide selection of world radio stations: just find one of the many sites that offer live radio links and choose the station that you want. (You will obviously need a sound card and a set of speakers or headphones in order to do this.) There are many advantages in listening to radio via the Internet: sound quality is usually superior (no reception problems to worry about), you can read descriptions of the various stations before you listen in to them, and you can switch easily between stations (no need to know the frequencies). The only disadvantages are the usual costs of being on-line and occasional problems with the delivery of the sound (this is done by a technique called *streaming*, whose efficiency relies on the speed and quality of your Internet connection). So good luck with your listening—there are lots of interesting stations out there in every language imaginable, and in no time at all you'll have your own personal favourites.

CD and Cassette

There is a wealth of foreign language material available on CD and cassette, with the added advantage that these media can be listened to in many different ways, e.g. home hi-fi systems, in-car players, portable stereos, multimedia computers, etc. This versatility means that you can listen to the foreign language at practically every point during the day, whether it's while jogging around the block, sitting in the car or waiting at the bus stop.

CD's and cassettes are also easy to store, quick to play and provide excellent sound quality; in short, they are ideal for language-learning purposes. Many local libraries (as well as those in educational institutions) now have large collections of audio materials, and it's well worth having a look to see if there's anything worth borrowing. If you prefer to buy, then there are numerous shops on the high street and on the Internet; all you need is the time to find what you're looking for and the funds to purchase it. Here are some suggestions regarding the types of CD's and cassettes that can help you learn a language:

- **Course and examination materials.** It may be that the course you are using comes with its own listening materials; if so, your teacher may be able to lend these to you. Similarly, if you are sitting a national examination that includes a listening element you may be able to access tapes or CD's of past papers.

- **Popular music.** Listening to albums and singles recorded in the foreign language can be an enjoyable way of extending your vocabulary. It helps if you have a copy of the song lyrics to read as you listen to the music—that way the words and their spellings will become fixed in your head along with the tune to which they are set.

- **Opera.** If you are a classical music fan, why not try listening to some opera in the language you are studying? You could either listen to individual pieces or entire operas, but make sure that you have the text in front of you—it can sometimes be difficult to make out singers clearly enough for you to understand them. A bonus point here is that opera CD's and tapes often include the original sung text along with an English translation.

- **Talking books.** These are a great way of reading in the foreign language. What I like to do is have the text (either in the foreign language or a translation) in front of me as I listen—it's amazing what you can learn from doing this.

- **Children's songs and nursery rhymes.** Despite being intended for young children, these can be a valuable source of listening practice. Once again it helps to be able to follow the words as you listen.

- **Poetry.** There are many excellent recordings of poetry available, often recited by famous actors. Hearing poems being read aloud can provide highly effective listening practice, as the pace of delivery is often slow, clear and expressive; as always, it helpful to have the text in front of you. The choice of poetry is also very important; try to avoid poems that are too complex and challenging, and choose those that are simple and direct (your teacher may be able to give you advice on this).

The Final Word

Let me leave you with this thought: how do you learn a language? The answer is simple: by using your *eyes* and *ears*. Right now you are probably thinking about what I have just said. Hold on—I haven't actually *said* it! It's you who have *read* it, and you have used your eyes to *see* the words and understand them. But if I had *said* it, then you would have used your ears to *hear* my words and understand them. (You might also be lucky enough to *see* me as you *hear* me, in which case my body language will help you understand my message.) If you then wanted to *speak* or *write* my words, you would have to *listen* to them or *see* them once again. That is the importance of *sound* and *vision*—without them, language learning is almost impossible. So take every opportunity to watch and listen, and you will be adequately rewarded.

People Power

Can you learn a language on your own? It's a good question, and one worth answering. In my opinion it is possible, but very difficult and I definitely don't recommend it. Just think about it; language is all about communication, and if you have nobody on whom to practise your language skills you're going to make very slow progress. Similarly, if you decide to teach yourself, then you have no-one to explain things to you and help you when you go wrong. I'm not saying that you won't make any progress by going it alone, but you are definitely making things difficult for yourself. You have to remember that learning a language is all about acquiring skills as well as knowledge.

Let me put it this way: if you knew absolutely nothing about driving and someone gave you a car, would you be able to learn by simply reading the information contained in a manual? The answer is yes; you could do it through trial and error, but it would take you a very long time and you would probably damage or crash the car in the process. Knowledge on its own is not quite enough, as you have to acquire the skills to put it into practice.

Learning a foreign language quickly and effectively involves getting the help and co-operation of other people, and to do this you have to make the effort to establish an effective relationship with them. If you don't, then you risk missing out on a lot of valuable linguistic interaction. Let's begin by listing these various people:

- Your teacher.

- Your fellow students and friends.

- Members of your family.

- Foreign language assistants.

- Foreign language tutors.

There may be others, but those that I have mentioned are by far the most important. We shall now consider each of them in turn, describing some of the various ways in which they can help you to learn a foreign language.

Your Teacher

It goes without saying that your teacher is the most important person in your language-learning life, and it is vital that you form and maintain a strong working relationship with him or her. Teaching and learning is very much a two-way process; the teacher monitors the responses of the student and modifies the teaching approach accordingly, while the student reacts to the teaching style by adapting his or her learning strategies. It is a relationship that involves a degree of give and take on both sides, and as a student you have to be prepared to take the initiative and show that you are ready to collaborate with your teacher. Try to put personalities to one side (both your own and the teacher's) and concentrate on the work that has to be done. (I say this because we are all human, and we can't always like one another!) The important thing is to have respect for your teacher and a professional attitude to your work; all teachers respond positively to this, and in the long run it makes everyone's job much easier.

What else can we do to ensure that we get the best out of our teacher? At this point I recommend that you read pages 23–24 of the chapter *Improve Your Learning Experience*, but here is a short summary of some of the most important pieces of advice:

- **Be proactive.** Work actively within the class by volunteering answers, asking questions, being generally alert to what is going on, always seeking to participate and encouraging others to do so.

- **Admit you need help.** Teachers are there to help you, so don't be ashamed to ask for assistance should you get into difficulty: most teachers will be delighted that you are prepared to do this.

- **Check your progress.** Get into the habit of asking your teacher how you are doing and how you can improve. Don't wait until those end of term reports!

Your Fellow Students

If you are studying your foreign language in the company of others, then you have a valuable opportunity to interact with your fellow students. Being in a class is like being part of a local community; the more neighbours that you make contact and communicate with, the better. By making the effort to introduce yourself and talk to others in your class, you will gradually build up a network of friends and acquaintances that in time can have a positive effect on your language studies. If you have good social skills and are outgoing and friendly, then you will enjoy doing this, whereas those of us who are much quieter and perhaps lack self-confidence will not find it so easy.

If this is the case, then you have to make an effort to overcome your shyness. Try to put yourself into situations where you can get to know as many of your classmates as possible; as I say to my students, *push yourself forward without being pushy*. Remember that going it alone is sometimes much more difficult than working with others; if you learn in isolation, then you miss out on the learning opportunities those around you can offer.

So how can you make the most of being with your fellow students within a classroom situation? Here are some ideas:

- **Make the most of paired and group activities.** Many foreign language activities involve working with one other person or in a group. You should ensure that you contribute fully on these occasions, as it's no use sitting back and letting others do the work; this is a two-way process, and for it to function properly there has to be genuine participation. If you do this, you will learn from others and others will learn from you—but only if you make the effort to communicate amongst yourselves. (For more advice on how to deal with group work, please read page 54.)

- **Collaborate with others.** Working with your fellow students doesn't always have to happen in class. There may be areas in the course where it can be to your advantage to work in this way, e.g. revision of past work, going over vocabulary, sharing notes, etc. That way learning becomes more enjoyable and effective, as you are interacting with someone at a similar stage and level to yourself.

A word of caution, however—try to avoid collaborating in areas where the teacher is expecting an individual response (e.g. essay work, grammar exercises, translations), as what inevitably happens is that everyone involved in the collaboration ends up with similar (if not identical) pieces of work. (As you can imagine, this is something that arouses suspicion in even the most trusting of teachers.)

- **Share your learning experiences.** It's good to talk to your fellow students about how you're finding the class. This can be on a daily basis, or whenever you feel like it—it doesn't really matter, as the important thing is to share your feelings and experiences with others. Think of it this way: you may find something difficult and come to the conclusion that it's your fault that you don't quite understand it. That's until you talk to other people after the class and find out that everyone has had the same problem!

Talking over things like this can be reassuring and sometimes a solution will present itself. If it doesn't (and the problem is a general one) then it's time for the class to have a word with their teacher. There is another aspect to this: every class is a collection of individuals, and not everyone will respond to a lesson in the same way. This means that by talking to others you can get a wide range of opinions and some new perspectives on your own learning experience. These can often be positive, as they encourage you to think about and evaluate your own performance and progress. So don't keep to yourself; get out there and start talking!

Your Family

As I have said elsewhere in this book, learning a foreign language doesn't stop when you're out of the classroom. What you do at home is just as important, whether it be homework, revision, learning vocabulary, etc. This is where your family can help you, especially if some of them are fluent in the language that you are studying. If this is the case, you can then enlist their help and expertise in these areas. If it isn't, then all is not lost; there are still ways in which family members with little or no active knowledge of the foreign language can be of assistance. All you have to do is to convince them that they are capable of helping you out in other ways. Here are a few suggestions:

- **Learning and reviewing vocabulary.** As you know, acquiring vocabulary is vital if you are going to progress in your language. Family members can help you by looking over the vocabulary lists that you have been learning and testing you orally on them—all they have to do is read out the words in English and ask you if you can remember them in the foreign language (they could also check your spellings).

- **Thinking up ideas.** On those occasions where you are preparing either an essay or a piece of extended speaking, it can be helpful to ask family members if they have any good ideas regarding content. They may be able to suggest things that you had never thought about, and that you might want to consider including in your work. Why limit yourself to your own imagination, when you can find inspiration in those around you?

If you were doing this as part of your work for the English class, then you might be accused of reproducing other people's ideas and passing them off as your own; but as a foreign language student, you still have to do the hard work of expressing these ideas in another language. So get into the habit of brainstorming with anyone in your family willing to help you out—you will get a whole new perspective on the task in hand.

One final point: it is often said that young people have greater imaginations that those who are older. Don't believe it! Parents and grandparents have an extra experience of life that puts them at a great advantage here, so make the most of their maturity and listen to what they have to say.

• **Sharing experiences.** You are probably not the first person in your family to have studied a foreign language. Parents, as well as elder brothers and sisters may well have done so in the past. If this is the case, talk to them about their experiences. Find out what they found interesting or boring, what their particular strengths and weaknesses were, what they felt about learning a language. The fact that it may all have happened a long time ago is irrelevant—the important thing here is to discuss their perceptions and recollections of learning a foreign language, even if they no longer remember a single word of it. That way you can draw comparisons with your own studies, and sometimes you will pick up useful tips and words of advice that can help you in the future.

There may also be members of your family who have spent some time in the country whose language you are studying; if so, talk to them about it. Remember that you cannot learn a language without knowing something about the country in which it spoken: its history, culture, traditions, customs and people. You can find this information in books or on the Internet (or even view it on television), but sometimes talking to someone who has been there can be much more interesting and informative, as you can question them directly about their experiences. You won't get the same depth of factual knowledge, but in its place you will hear a first-hand account that will teach you more.

• **Keep them posted.** It is a good idea to keep family members up to date regarding your progress in the foreign language. Show them examples of work you have done, and discuss your classroom experiences regularly. Talk openly and regularly about your triumphs and failures, and about what you hope to achieve in the future. This way, you stand a good chance of receiving help, advice and encouragement, all of which will help you to become a better learner into the bargain. (One further advantage: there will be no surprises when your teacher delivers that long-awaited progress report!)

The Foreign Language Assistant

Many educational institutions employ foreign language assistants to help classes with their learning. These are normally young students from the country whose language you are studying, and who are spending time abroad as part of their university courses in order to improve their English. If you are lucky enough to have access to a foreign language assistant, then you should make the most of the excellent opportunities this offers. A good way of doing this is to make sure that you fully understand the role of the foreign language assistant, and how they can best help you with your studies. Here are some points to bear in mind:

- **Acquaint yourself with the job.** The foreign language assistant is there to ensure that you have regular contact with a native speaker. He or she will either work alongside the classroom teacher or independently with small groups of students, and may only be available at certain times. There are many different kinds of activities that foreign language assistants get involved in: oral work, listening comprehension, reading aloud, vocabulary building, producing new teaching materials, etc. They also provide students with a clear link to the foreign country and its language, as well as being a useful point of reference for teachers. We should always bear in mind, however, that foreign language assistants are *not* trained teachers, and so it would be unfair of us to expect them to behave as such.

- **Maximise your involvement.** It's up to you, the student, to ensure that you participate fully in any activities involving the foreign language assistant. This is particularly important if you are working on your own or in a small group, and independently of your teacher. In these situations the foreign language assistant will be on their own, and will need positive and lively feedback from you if they are to succeed in their task. Don't make life difficult for them—respond at every opportunity, and show that you are interested in what they are saying and doing. Talk as much as you can to them in the foreign language, and make every moment count by telling yourself this simple fact: *Here I am face to face with a native speaker, and if I don't make the effort now, I never will.*

Sometimes you may find that you have difficulty understanding the foreign language assistant. If this is the case, then don't be afraid to ask them to slow down and/or rephrase what they are saying; remember that they may be unaware that they are causing problems, and are relying on you to put them on the right path. As for yourself, you will find that your level of comprehension will improve the more time you spend with the foreign language assistant, with the result that he or she will eventually be able to speak completely naturally to you, and you will understand every word.

- **Expand your learning.** Encourage your foreign language assistant to go beyond the language taught in class. Find out about their background and their interests, and get them talking about the things that are important to them in their lives—all in the foreign language, of course! You might want to get together with your fellow students and organise extra conversation classes outside class time; these can provide excellent oral practice in a relaxed and informal setting. Much depends, of course, on the personality of your foreign language assistant and the degree to which they are willing to get involved in such extracurricular activities, but in my experience most are only too happy to do so.

Foreign Language Tutors

It would be wrong to assume that learning a foreign language is a straightforward and simple task that anyone can carry out without the slightest trouble. The reality is that we are all individuals, with different strengths and weaknesses, learning in different ways and at different rates; because of this, we very rarely encounter the same difficulties. For some it is one particular skill (such as listening, speaking, reading or writing) that causes trouble, whereas for others it is understanding grammar or acquiring vocabulary.

Your first port of call when you are having difficulties should be your teacher. All good teachers will be only to happy to help out, perhaps by spending some extra time with you or setting you supplementary work for you to do on your own. Sometimes, however, you may feel that you need some continuous professional support outside of your normal classes. One possible solution is to pay for extra tuition: the advantages of this system is that you get one-to-one coaching at a time and place convenient to yourself, and you can ask your tutor to cover the precise areas in which you are having difficulty. Finding a tutor can sometimes be difficult, although there are now specialised agencies that can provide one. I would suggest, however, that you first ask your teacher for advice. Sometimes he or she will be prepared to tutor you personally; if not, they might be able to put you in touch with other teachers who offer this service. One other possibility is foreign language assistants, as they are often quite willing to earn some extra cash by tutoring students.

The big disadvantage of paying for extra tuition is the on-going costs, which can be quite high. One alternative is to enrol in a night-class; you will probably still have to pay, but the costs are often lower. This option works quite well if you can find a suitable class in your area, but bear in mind that you will be part of a group of people—perfect if it's extra practice that you are looking for, but not so great if you need individual attention.

Finally, don't overlook what your place of learning may be able to offer you. Many teaching institutions are now running homework and supported study classes that students can attend in their own time. (A word of explanation: homework classes allow you to do homework not at home, but at your place of learning and are supervised by a teacher who can help you if required. Supported study classes are run by individual departments as a supplement to the official course, often during the period before examinations.) If your place of learning hasn't organised anything like this, then you should take the initiative and ask them to consider it—my experience of these classes is that they are very worthwhile, and if you can you should certainly give them a try.

The Final Word

All the people I have talked about in this chapter have one thing in common: the ability to influence and shape your language learning for the better. However, this can only happen if you take the time and effort to establish and maintain positive relationships with them. As we have seen, they can all contribute something to your learning, but only if you allow them to do so. Therefore it's up to you to communicate clearly and constantly, so that everyone is aware of your concerns, difficulties and needs.

Remember that the most successful linguists learn not only from books, but from individuals. They are never too proud to ask for help if they require it, nor arrogant in assuming that they have nothing left to learn. They show enterprise and persistence in involving others in their learning, and are grateful and appreciative of the assistance they receive. If this is you, then congratulations—you have realised that you cannot learn a language in isolation. If it isn't, then act on the advice I've given you, and make the most of *people power*.

Getting Abroad

Question: what is the best way of improving your language skills? Answer: spend some time in the country whose language you are studying. If you're not convinced, then I suggest that you take a little time to consider the advantages. Here are a few of them:

- Being in the foreign country places you within a different culture and lifestyle; you can meet new people, experience their way of life and thus expand your own horizons.

- You have almost unlimited opportunities to listen to, speak, read and write the foreign language by interacting with other people and/or media.

- Time spent in the foreign country is highly valued by future educators and employers, and demonstrates that you are a resourceful and enterprising student.

- On a personal level, the periods we spend abroad are often the most formative, memorable and fulfilling of our lives.

If you're still doubtful, then don't give up reading this chapter; there are many different ways of spending time abroad, and one of them may well appeal to you. It is important, however, that you evaluate your own reasons for wanting to spend time in a foreign country, and that you do this before looking at the various options available to you. Here are some questions that you might ask yourself:

- What exactly do I want to achieve from my stay?

- How will the type of stay I am considering help me to fulfil my objectives?

- How am I going to make sure that I meet those objectives?

- How long do I intend to stay abroad?

- Where exactly do I want to go?

- Have I considered the financial implications of my stay?

- Am I old and mature enough to cope with being abroad?

- Is my family happy about it?

You may find it helpful to discuss the above questions with an older person (such as a parent, teacher or student advisor), as they can check that you have considered all the different aspects of going abroad and are not doing it for the wrong reasons. They may also be able to offer good, practical advice, in addition to pointing out other opportunities and possibilities of which you might be unaware. Once you have established what it is that you would like to do, you then have to look closely at the different types of stay that may be available to you.

Types of Stay

There are basically two types of stay: those that you organise yourself or with your family, and those that are organised for you by your place of learning. Here are some examples of both:

- **Holidays.** These are probably the most straightforward types of stay to organise, as you have complete control over all the arrangements: where you will be going and for how long, how you're going to get there, who will be accompanying you, and what you'll be doing when you get there. You can choose between short package breaks or decide to organise your own travel and accommodation. You may also be able to access the many reduced fares available to young people and students. Bear in mind, however, that the costs may still be quite high; one way of getting around this is to persuade your family to have a holiday in the country whose language you are studying and take you along with them. One possible problem about arranging a holiday as a way of practising your language skills is that being in the company of family and/or friends can lead you to talk more English than might be desirable, but you can make sure that you get plenty oral practice in the foreign language by offering your services as an interpreter.

- **Trips Organised by Educational Institutions.** These allow students the opportunity to experience the foreign country through a programme of visits and activities that put the emphasis firmly on language learning and practice.

Trips of this type are often subsidised so as to reduce the overall cost to students, with all your travel arrangements being made by the organisers. The fact that your teachers accompany you is a great advantage, as you can refer to them if you need help or get into difficulty. They will also ensure that you get the most out of your stay, by placing you in situations where you will be able to use your language skills. Most educational institutions regularly organise trips abroad for their students; if this isn't the case, have a word with your teacher.

- **Student Exchanges.** These can be an excellent way of spending time in the foreign country. This is how it works: your place of learning arranges for a group of you to be paired off with a similar group at a place of learning abroad. You then get to know your partner by writing or e-mailing to them over a period of time, or by collaborating on some institution-based project. When the time arrives for the exchange, you each spend some time in each other's country. For example, the first leg of the exchange might involve the foreign group coming over to your own country for a few weeks, accompanied by their teachers. During that time they would attend classes at your place of learning and take part in leisure and sightseeing activities organised for them. You would also be expected to host your partner in your own home for the duration of the stay and spend time with them in the evening and at weekends. (The language of communication at this stage would be English.)

When it is time for the second leg to take place, you then travel to the foreign country with your fellow students and teachers for exactly the same experience, but this time in reverse: you are the one staying at your partner's home and attending the foreign place of learning, and so you have to use the foreign language almost all the time. The advantages of taking part in an exchange are obvious: you can live with a family abroad, get to know another person of the same age but of different nationality, attend a place of learning in another country, acquaint yourself with a new culture, and improve your language knowledge and skills immeasurably. The costs of participating in an exchange are often less than for other types of stays abroad as they tend to attract a lot of funding from outside bodies, thereby reducing the cost to students.

A variation on the student exchange described above is one that involves yourself and one other person only. This will usually be a pen-friend or e-mail correspondent with whom you have been in touch for some time and know quite well, with the next step being to get both families to agree to a home stay in each of your respective countries. The main advantage of a one-to-one exchange is that you have complete control over timing and duration (something that does not happen with a student exchange); furthermore, you and your partner can plan exactly how you are going to spend your time in each other's country. So if you get the chance to take part in either type of exchange, go for it—it can be a wonderful opportunity that is impossible to repeat when you are older.

- **Language Courses.** There is a wide range of language courses available abroad, offered for the most part by universities, colleges and language schools. The great advantage of this mode of study is its flexibility: you decide on the length and the timing of the course, which can be either on a full or part-time basis. You can also choose between working in a class with other students, or having one-to-one tuition tailored to your own needs and specifications. Some class-based courses ask you to sit a language proficiency examination to gauge your ability level, whereas others accept documentary evidence. The content of courses varies enormously; some offer complete language learning programmes, while others focus on developing individual skills. Many also include a cultural element, with classes on the art, music and literature of the country whose language you are studying.

  Language courses abroad can obviously be an excellent way of improving your knowledge and skills, but selecting the right course can often be difficult. Try to get advice and recommendations from either your teacher or other students who have attended similar courses (the Internet can be an excellent source of such information). Read any promotional literature carefully, paying especial attention to the small print. Make sure that you know what the precise costs will be: fees, accommodation, subsistence, travel, etc. Once you find a course that you think is suitable, enquire about the possibility of getting funding; your teacher or student adviser may be able to inform you of any grants and bursaries that may be available.

- **Work Experience.** Many educational institutions are now organising periods of work experience abroad for their students. These are often the result of collaboration between the science, technical and information technology departments and local companies with a presence in overseas markets. They are therefore most suited to students who are studying one or more of these subjects along with a foreign language, and who intend pursuing future careers in these areas. Alternatively, there are many schemes that combine a stay in the foreign country with some casual work experience (e.g. working in a restaurant or bar), and are therefore not vocationally orientated. Accommodation in both types of scheme is normally provided by host families, an arrangement that maximises the opportunities for students to speak the foreign language. Some student exchanges also contain a work experience element that can supplement or replace the time normally spent in the classroom.

Finally, if you are about to leave your place of learning to continue your language studies at an institute of higher education, then why not delay for a year and use the time to work abroad? (This is known as a *gap year*, and is becoming an increasingly popular option amongst students who wish to expand their horizons before settling down to a period of final and extended study.) Gap years are especially suited to work experience abroad because of the longer time-frame, and there are many organisations that can help with the practical aspects of finding employment and accommodation.

- **Voluntary Service.** This option is one that attracts many young people, as it offers them the possibility of helping those less fortunate than themselves. Because of its nature, it is limited to students aged eighteen or over, and consequently is a popular choice for gap years. Working within a local community in the foreign country is obviously a highly effective way of improving your oral skills, but you should bear in mind that it can be difficult, tiring and emotionally draining. There are many projects on offer world-wide: these range from summer work camps of two to four weeks' duration to full-scale placements within social welfare, environmental and educational programmes lasting between three and twelve months. Once again grants may be available to young people wishing to participate.

Making the Most of Your Stay

Once you get to the foreign country, your main objective should be to ensure that you maximise every linguistic opportunity that comes along; after all, if you waste your time when you're abroad you won't be able to make amends when you get back home. Your stay in the foreign country may be the only chance you will have to perfect your knowledge and skills, so think carefully about how you are going to achieve this.

It's all too easy when we are abroad to sit back and relax, especially in countries where the weather, food, sights and amusements are all much better than at home; before we know it we are in holiday mode, and the days and weeks slip by without any real linguistic involvement on our part. This is fine if we *are* on holiday (in which case we deserve a little rest and relaxation), but the point I'm trying to make is that are always opportunities to practise your language skills whatever your reason for being abroad. So it doesn't matter if you are on an exchange trip, a language course or doing voluntary service—the fact that you are in the foreign country should be enough to spur you into action. What should you be doing? Read on for some useful suggestions:

- **Talk as much as you can.** It's no use being abroad and avoiding situations where you have to talk to people. Try to be friendly and outgoing; make the effort to converse with others, and don't be afraid to try out new phrases and expressions you may have learnt. Don't get too hung up about the content and accuracy of what you are saying; the important thing is to get across your message, even if it isn't word perfect. If you don't succeed the first time, then try again. Persistence will eventually pay off, and the reward is the confidence boost that comes when you realise that the other person has understood and appreciated what you have said. After all, most people will admire you for making the effort to speak their language, as it doesn't always happen in a world that is becoming increasingly dominated by English.

- **Conduct your transactions in the foreign language.** For example, when you go shopping don't always take the easy way out and head for the local supermarket; after all, there's very little talking to be done when you're placing your purchases in a trolley. Try out the local shops, where you'll be served and will have to explain exactly what you want. Alternatively, try a street market where you might even get the opportunity to haggle over the price. When you buy bus or railway tickets or change money in a bank, take advantage of the situation to ask some pertinent questions (even if you already know the answers!). That way you'll give yourself plenty openings in which to practise the language. Here's another idea; stop a local to ask the way to somewhere. It may be that you already have a good idea of how to get there, but the directions you receive will be excellent listening practice. If you don't understand them, then you can always ask again!

- **Live like the locals.** When you're in a foreign country, it pays to follow the regional customs and to try to fit in to the way of living. It's unlikely, of course, that you'll ever do this so well as to be mistaken for one of the inhabitants, but adapting your lifestyle to your surroundings can teach you a lot about the country and its language. For example, try to eat and drink in the same way as the locals—if you're dining out, go to a restaurant serving local cuisine rather than to the nearby Macdonald's. (Think about it—you can eat plenty hamburgers when you get home!) When somebody offers to buy you a drink, try something local rather than stick to your usual choice. If there is a street festival on, then get out there and take part. The trick is to get involved in as many aspects of local life as you can; if you do this, you will earn the respect and approval of the resident population, as well as broaden your own perceptions and understanding of a different culture. It's all summed up in this famous saying: *When in Rome, do as the Romans do.*

- **Record your stay.** It makes good sense to have a visual, aural and written record of your stay in the foreign country. Why not keep a diary in which you recount your daily experiences? You could also note down any new and interesting vocabulary, expressions and information that you come across and would like to access in the future. Another good idea is to take photographs of people, places and things that interest you and then annotate them in the foreign language; alternatively, take some video and either add your own foreign language commentary or film people talking to one another. If you do something like this regularly you will end up with a written and/or audio-visual archive that will be of great value to you, both as a record of your stay and as a study resource. If you don't have a video-camera, then you could always make live audio recordings of conversations, but be careful to ask people's permission before attempting to do this.

- **Use the local media.** Try to watch as much television as possible, even if you're not too keen on what they're showing—it's listening to the foreign language that counts. The same goes for radio programmes and watching films at the local cinema; both are excellent sources of spoken language. If you can afford it, buy as many newspapers and magazines as you have the time to read in depth; you won't always understand every word, but you'll never fail to learn something!

The Final Word

Going abroad is the icing on the cake as far as learning a foreign language is concerned. It is still possible to be a very good linguist without ever going near the foreign country, so if your financial or personal circumstances make it difficult or impossible to get abroad at the moment, then don't despair—you can still achieve great things if you put your mind to it. Learning a language is a lifelong activity, and there will be plenty of opportunities in the future.

If, on the other hand, you are lucky enough to be able to participate in some of the activities I have described in this chapter, then ensure that you make every moment count. Time abroad is precious, and should never be wasted. Use it wisely, and you will become not only a better linguist, but a better and more tolerant person. Many years ago Ralph Waldo Emerson, the famous American writer, wrote on this very subject: *No doubt, to a man of sense, travel offers advantages. As many languages as he has, as many friends, as many arts and trades, so many times is he a man. A foreign country is a point of comparison, wherefrom to judge his own.* The same is true today, and will be for the students of tomorrow. In the meantime it's up to you to make your stay abroad a reality. Good luck, and *bon voyage* when the time comes!

0-595-31933-5